The
Big Herbs

An awesome read, this is the remarkable story of a farmer, a farm and a piece of land loved back to life. With simple words and powerful imaginary, all true and straight from the heart, Paul shares his deeply personal story of living life fully, taking risks, standing tall for what you believe in, and loving the earth passionately. Reading *The Big Herbs* is as close as one could get to hiking through the woodlands with Paul, trying to keep up with a man who can teach, dig, weed, plant, and story tell all in one big breath.

Between this book and the film made about his life's work, *Sanctity of Sanctuary,* Paul's message is preserved for future generations. I'm imagining one day that people will be looking up Paul Strauss in the Smithsonian or Museum of Appalachian Folklore, or at the Jim Duke Welcoming Center at Golden Seal Sanctuary, and find archived there these stories of his life and life work.

Rosemary Gladstar, herbalist and author

The Big Herbs

The Use and Abuse,
Natural History and Identification
of Major Tree and Shrub Species
in the MidWest and Eastern U.S.,
with Stories and Insights
of a Life Married to Farm and Forest

Paul Strauss

XOXOX
PRESS

Library of Congress Cataloguing in Publication Data

Strauss, Paul, 1950-
  The big herbs : the use and abuse, natural history and identification of major tree and shrub species in the Midwest and Eastern U.S. with stories and insights of a life married to farm and forest / Paul Strauss. -- 1st ed.
      p. cm.
  Includes bibliographical references and index.
  ISBN 978-1-880977-36-1 (alk. paper)
  1. Medicinal plants--Ohio--Meigs County. 2. Trees--Ohio--Meigs County. 3. Trees--Therapeutic use. 4. Organic farmers--Ohio--Meigs County--Biography. 5. Herbalists--Ohio--Meigs County--Biography. 6. Strauss, Paul, 1950- I. Title.
  QK99.U6S77 2013
  581.6'340977199--dc23
                    2013030221

My Thanks

Carl, I never ran into you again after time spent around Taos. Did you ever make it back to Canada and settle on your peoples' land? I wonder about your good life often. Thanks and big respect, you opened the door—Love and deep gratitude to Bill Clonch for his teaching and friendship and energy, and his suggestion that maybe I should buy that farm on McCumber Hill Road with the big cave on it—The Wood family, who made me feel loved and welcome as a very young man in this foreign land and gave me a chance to work on their farm—These friends who became my family gave me the tools I needed to find the right road and navigate this earthly life—Deep thanks to Jamey Jones and Alana Galt-Theis, who have taken my words from pencil to computer and filled my life with love—I was going to self-publish this book, but then I met Jerry Kelly, who shared the task gratefully—Thanks Rosi for the tears in the Goldenseal—To Wendy Minor Viny for the photo-montages herein, a talented & devoted artist whom I'm lucky to know as a neighbor. To all those herbalists and friends who gave their time and money to raise a sanctuary—and of course to my main mule Jerry who had the patience to put up with me 'til my skills caught up with his. I think of you every day—And all the dogs, so many of you, who kept me company walking these hills in our own heaven—*We wear no stinking leashes.* All thanks and amazement at the deep knowledge of our First Nation People and their thousands of years living with the plants and animals with respect, the only way—Gratitude to all those friends who were brave enough to buy land here, to live a green life and help create an amazing community, a sane place in these times.

P.S., Rutland Ohio, August 2013

"A life centered on the earth is the most rewarding, giving you opportunities to view the interconnection of all things and the dancing circles of life and death, to be endlessly humbled and amazed as you reap what you sow."

Contents

Paul and Kiya, who was three-quarters wolf, 1986.
Note the handful of Calendula for Golden Salve.

—*Prologue*—

"What I know as the Divine Science and Holy Scripture I learnt in the woods and fields. I have no other master than the Beeches and Oaks. Listen to a man of experience, thou wilt learn more in the woods than books. Trees and stones will teach thee more than thou canst acquire from the mouth of a Magister."—Saint Bernard

Being a lazy student, having always had an impossible time with indoor classrooms and studies, reports and tests—indoor-about-anything—I am a devotee of the Saint's words. Some may find a balance between the academic interior world and outdoor activities…I never have. I am not a natural writer but so admire those who have the discipline to write and study for long hours and days. I find it arduous and would rather be working in the woods or gardens, even building fence. I just have to get dirty to feel my connection to this life.

My writing beach.
Photo courtesy Alana Galt-Theis

The majority of the content of this book was written in pencil on a hard-to-reach Hawaiian beach under the shade of a Kiawe tree, over a period of seven years. In this place my daily work would be kayaking or surfing, hiking, shelling, snorkeling and swimming, often with hump-back whales, spinner dolphins and green sea turtles. These are some important things my farm does not provide. But for pond swimming, I do not have close access to the water bounty that helps balance my intense farm life. But I do get to this beach most winters for a month or so, and stuff myself with ocean. It is then easy to eat, relax, read, write, think, and take a break from my 11-month job on the farm while it's in Ohio's winter dormancy. It's here I've written most of *The Big Herbs* while connecting the dots of this amazing earth and this good life.

Being able to write this book has been a long but enjoyable way to pass on The Green Spark and reach others, especially the young—to let them know that there is a different way to live and think than the current model. The earth could use you now. It is good to share all that our multi-species forests provide, and advocate for their sane use and protection. I hope these words, experiences, and insights of a life married to a farm and forest might be thought-provoking enough to change lives. I would love to have found such a book at a young age. *Living the Good Life* by Helen and Scott Nearing did inspire me in my early teenage years and I am grateful to them for that.

In the scheme of things, the last 42 years on this farm are barely a drop in the bucket of time and history, but in the scale of a human life they are a large chunk. The farm is my classroom and my teacher, and I never graduate. It also happens to be my business, my food and water source, my heat source, my drugstore, and my inspiration, all wrapped into one.

Over the past years there have been big changes for the good here, and of course, some for the bad. The 80 acres I originally bought had never been strip-mined but some of the surrounding farms were in the early 1950s. Human greed, carelessness and short sight-edness seem to play a major part of our shared human history. These areas were not reclaimed for 40 years. You know the human pattern of take/take, profit being a major life motive at all costs for so many. It's a pattern that does not value the sanctity and protection of our earth.

When I moved here in 1970/1971, not an insect—let alone a fish, frog, turtle, or mink—lived in the creek. Acid mine runoff had killed all life in it. Surrounding parts of the old farms looked like the moon with garbage. Back then, to see a deer was a wondrous event; it is common now. Bobcats were not even a thought back then, but they're back, as are bear sightings. Turkey did not even exist here then, they are everywhere now. Raccoons, squirrels, groundhogs, and opossum populations, though noticeable back in the seventies, are far more numerous now. We did have a songbird population then, but now it has doubled, maybe more.

But even then, down in the deep hollers there were the herbs, large populations of hundreds of species, a veritable botanical ark. The big old timber was selectively cut over the past 150 years, but there are still some old ones left, along with thousands of acres of mature forest. Next to me and the United Plant Savers Botanical Sanctuary, on Joe and Wendy Viny's property, there is still some old growth that is protected and will never be cut. And those herbs down in all our hollers are absolutely going crazy, taking over the place. Our creeks are again full of insects, turtles, frogs, fish, and mink.

It's a good story. Finally reclamation took place in the 80s by the government and also by me on the acres of land I bought to protect the forest and watershed. We now have a young, like-minded community who have bought up many of the local farms around me, thousands of acres. And of course there is the United Plant Savers Botanical Sanctuary (aka The Goldenseal Sanctuary), the first sanctuary in the United States dedicated to at-risk medicinal plants. Hard to believe in Meigs County, Ohio, known more for the extractive industries of coal mining and logging, along with deer hunting, tomato farming, and marijuana cultivation, we now have something that has always been here to be very proud of, a herbal botanical ark worth protecting and promoting.

As a means of simple, local conservation, for there is more land to protect than I can handle, I have encouraged many friends, interns, and students to purchase land when it comes up for sale in the neighborhood. I have also sold a few parcels from my farm. It is nice to know that herbology and farm life—besides being simply self-sustaining and self-fulfilling—have the ability to protect land and build community. At the same time, because of my relationship with botany professors at Ohio University in Athens, I have allowed and encouraged many students to access this land for their Masters theses. Oh, and in no way am I the leader of this community. Every one of these families has The Green Spark and has figured out their own way to live green on the land. I was only here first and it was evident to me that conservation of this bountiful herbal land was of prime importance.

I have always been a truly spoiled herbalist. I've taken my good luck—having access to so many important medicinal plants—for granted. As I have our plethora of food and survival herbs. It's just the way it is. I know Bill Clonch took it for granted. Being spoiled is good when it can do good for all.

My understanding about just how spoiled I was took place about twenty years ago while teaching with herbalist Rosemary Gladstar. Rosie has served as a conduit for herbalists everywhere for a long time. Her teachings have taken her far and wide and have positively impacted so many. I also have been doing this plant work for a long time, but more localized because it took a long and concentrated effort to acquire the skills I needed to rebuild this particular farm and forest. Rosie and I were taking a long hike through the land that would become the UpS Botanical Sanctuary, walking through the area now called Hydrastis Heaven because of its abundance of the miraculous plant Goldenseal, not to mention big populations of Black and Blue Cohosh, Trillium, Virginia Snakeroot, Hepatica, Wild Ginger, and Bloodroot, all so thick and high it was impossible not to step on some of them. I noticed Rosemary was missing. I knew she was loving and appreciating the walk on this beautiful summer day and I couldn't imagine where she was. So I took the time to backtrack and found Rosie kneeling and weeping in the thickest stands of Goldenseal. It truly was a beautiful sight, this amazing herbalist totally surrounded by Goldenseal. The stand is so thick I could only see her head, as if Rosemary was being swallowed up by Goldenseal. How perfect! But I can admit I copped an attitude and said "What's going on, Rosemary?" Rosemary looked up at me with her large tear-filled dark eyes and says, "Do you know what you have here?" My comment back was something like, "Yeah, a lot of freaking Goldenseal." And Rosemary's response leading to my needed lesson was, "This is soooo rare." In that moment I knew just how terribly spoiled I was. I've been laughing at myself ever since.

Later on it became obvious that we needed to turn this land into a botanical sanctuary. Rosemary had just formed the organization United Plant Savers, which is dedicated to protecting At-Risk native medicinal plants. I became a member of the board of directors of UPS and my dear friend and Naturopath Richard Liebmann became its first director.

It is one thing to think about making a piece of land a botanical sanctuary but it is a much bigger task to purchase it and make it happen. Talk is cheap. One of the methods we used to accomplish this goal was to hold an herb conference on this land in September of that year. Many people attended the conference that day, including all of the UPS board members who gave so much time and effort to make it possible. Our ultimate goal was to figure out a way to purchase the property.

The conference was a great success, every person who attended it was totally floored by the monstrous herbal bounty of this special property. Richard had gotten in touch with Michael and Judy Funk, who owned a large and very successful natural foods distributorship in California. At the end of the day, I remember it clearly, it was a very dry September, Richard, Michael, Rosemary, and myself were taking a walk right down the rock bottom of Main Holler Creek, which was mostly dry. Rosemary and I were twenty yards ahead of Richard and Michael and totally engaged in talking about the abundance of plants around us and the success of the conference. We were walking to the West and there were clouds in the sky. Near the end of our walk the sun broke through the cloud cover and illuminated the area all around us in a ball of golden light. I turned around to make sure Michael and Richard were aware of the beauty of being surrounded by light, a phenomena I call light holes. I could see that Richard and Michael were engaged in deep conversation and right above their heads, maybe four feet above Michael's head, was a group of perfectly ripe Pawpaws, absolutely glowing in the light. Earlier that day, when talking to Michael, I had mentioned the abundance of Pawpaws on the property and he told me that being a Westerner he had never tasted a fresh Pawpaw and always wanted to try one. The moment was set. I broke into their conversation and alerted Michael that right above his head were large, ripe Pawpaws, at which point we of course picked them and give Michael his first taste of this unique and delicious native fruit. As Michael ate his first taste of this sweet soft custard-like fruit a smile formed on the corners of his Pawpaw covered mouth. I have always felt that these light holes are temporary transformational moments and whenever I see them I immediately stop what I'm doing and get in them to be bathed by the light. An hour later, Michael generously gave us the money we needed to finish purchasing the UpS Botanical Sanctuary. Magic does happen. This event is forever apart of the UPS history and is referred to as The Magic Pawpaw Moment.

Even with all this earthly abundance, there are many problematic issues around here today. Many farms are now being clear-cut for pulp to burn at coal-fired power plants, something American Electric Power is calling "green energy." And there is always the specter in this energy crazed world of re-coal-mining, which we have already had to battle, and of course large scale gas and oil drilling (Hydraulic Fracking). Luckily, our area doesn't seem to have the geology to destroy this land again. Even so, toxic fracking water is being brought here from out of state to be put into local injection wells, and even though power plants are putting on scrubbers, airborne pollution can always be a problem. The advance of invasive species is terribly alarming and widespread now because of international trade and abandoned farm land and human beings being unaware or not caring about it. We lost our American Chestnut years ago; Dogwood is in decline; Slippery and American

Elm are succumbing to Dutch Elm Tree Disease and Elm Phloem Necrosis; Ash trees may be wiped out in the next twenty years due to the Emerald Ash Borer that came here from trade with China; and Sudden Oak Death Syndrome seems to be hitting our Oak populations. The Asian Long-horned Beetle is now in Ohio and will negatively affect many tree species. The Woolly Adelgid from Asia is starting to destroy our Hemlock population. Our Butternut, Walnut, and Basswood populations have been drastically reduced by logging. Invasive species such as Shrub Honeysuckle, Autumn Olive, Garlic Mustard, Multiflora Rose and Japanese Stilt Grass have moved into large tracks of fields and forests unabated. What will our forests and farms look like in twenty years? What will my daughters and their young friends have left?

What can you do to help? If you want to change the world for the better start locally…

Plant native trees and prairies. This is common knowledge. It has been a wonderful success in Kenya, find the story of Wangari Maathai who won a Nobel Peace Prize in 2004 for her tree planting in Kenya. Trees meet so many needs at once: they give oxygen; eat CO_2; clean the air; are a sane source of local building materials; give heat; provide food and medicine; increase insect, bird, and all wildlife populations; and provide erosion control.

Buy and protect abandoned farms and forest. We have reasonable land prices in Appalachia and amazing botany.

Join local organizations like United Plant Savers (www.unitedplantsavers.org, 802-476-6467) and Buckeye Forest Council (buckeyeforestcouncil.org, 614-487-9290).

Take your children and friends into the woods and fields and teach them about our precious botanical and biological bounty.

Consider becoming a UPS intern. Contact Chip Carroll (740)742-1111 or go onto the UPS website, unitedplantsavers.org

Be aware and destroy invasive species. Contact Rural Action (http://ruralaction.org or call 740-677-4047)

Educate your neighbors and offer to help them

"Be the change you want to see in this world" –Gandhi

Live simply and grow as much of your food as you can. Confront your consumption and vote with your money. Consider the social, environmental, and biological implications of every purchase. **Make a difference**.

Be aware. Out of all the humans who have ever lived throughout all history and time—over 5,000 generations—our lives now are blessed to have choice and bounty and peace. Make no mistake, this is just not so in all of America and much of this world today. Don't take choice and bounty and peace for granted. Give thanks and give as much as you take.

Golden Healing Salve in different stages of setting up.
Photo by Paul Strauss

Part-I
—Conceiving Sanctuary—

Illustration by Wendy Minor Viny

—1—
Wood Musings

Finally the season's first real cold snap…strong winds, high temperature of 25°, frozen ground. The sheep and donkeys are more insistent for their morning grain, song birds are ready for their feeders to be filled. I let Little Spot in, as her small beagle body can't stay warm in these cold conditions. A good day to commune with the new woodstove…think, dream, write, plan, and of course, rest.

I don't know why it took me so long (33 years) to embrace some of the newer wood burning technology. I love my old stove; it proved itself in some heavy winters keeping this 140-year old home warm. It became obvious that there was more to consider than just heat; the old Free Flow never had ash pans to make for an easier clean-out and subsequently, a cleaner house. The new stove is fitted with a smoke re-burner (not a catalytic converter), making for cleaner air and creating less creosote buildup. And most wonderful are the large, glass windows set in the heavy cast doors—giving a magnificent view of the release of accumulated solar energy. How much I have missed, for so long, without stove glass! Yes, it may seem pitiful to some, but I know the story, species, and area of the property that every piece of wood comes from, and I know the circumstances that led each piece of wood I burn to my stove. Each burns with its own signature.

The morning's Sassafras log felled by last February's storm had already been weakened by heart rot. Sassafras catches easily and burns hot, its oil creates snapping flames of different colors. On top of Sassafras' hot coals, I put chunks of White Oak and Osage. These species burn hot, but will be there for hours burning slow, real slow, like the Oak grew. The massive White Oak, seven feet in diameter, grew for 250-plus years on the fence line between my and my neighbors Joe and Wendy Viny's property. The old Oak saw a lot in that time, certainly the native encampments down by the creek below the small cave, where I find arrowheads, small knives, and scrapers. She gave it up in 60 mph frontline winds in a beautiful July thunderstorm. Her falling took out the Osage beneath her 30-foot horizontal limbs.

The Oak was there before fence lines, witness to centuries of native families gathering her acorns. How many squirrels, deer, turkey, and bear, have also come to gather your manna. Even in death, she was still giving warmth and reflection and deep appreciation in such a worthy life…a perfect passing.

When my mind thinks of the eastern deciduous forest, the first species I see is White Oak and of course, Goldenseal. To me, they are royalty. I could go on and on about the White Oaks myriad giving from medicine to utility, but that is in another article in this book. Try reading, *Oak: The Frame of Civilization* by William Bryant Logan (Norton Press). Watch out—you might fall in love.

The Osage or "Bow Wood" is even heavier than White Oak. With its milky sap, it burns with intense heat and popping. Its wood will even outlast Black Locust for fencing or any outdoor building. Bill taught me to use its wood to make the single trees and the double trees I needed for the mules. It's like vegetable steel.

I think about time more now, with my life swiftly approaching a 60/40 reality check—60 years on the planet, 40 on the farm. Time has finally given me an ever-present awareness and appreciation of this forest I live in and the myriad species within it. I'm thinking of the many ways I use this forest, and I laugh at the ghastly sound when it's brought down to the reality of utility. Yet still it keeps on giving after such abuse. These trees know my reverence and impermanence, and tolerate me. My life would not be my life without this forest.

I consume their flower, fruits, and nuts
(Redbud, Persimmon, Hickory, Pawpaw)

Their dead bodies heat my home
(Oak, Locust, Hickory, Sassafras)

I bury their butts to build fences
(Locust and Osage)

I chop and grind them into medicines
(Slippery Elm, Blackhaw, White Oak, Black Walnut, Goldenseal)

I mulch with their leaves
(Maple)

My bees rob their nectar and steal their pollen
(Poplar, Maple, Elm)

I mill their fallen bodies into lumber through which I pound nails
(Ash, Oak, Poplar)

Month of Moon in Flat Tire

There is nothing like coming back to one's farm after a winter's absence. That old comfortable familiarity combined with a sense of rediscovery is a peak life experience. I am lovingly mauled by my dogs, who have patiently waited for their boy since mid-January. Do you know the bumper sticker, "Lord make me as good as my dogs think I am"? I have lived with horses, mules, donkeys, cows, goats, sheep, and chickens who consider me their friend, but their emotions are cooler, more subdued than my canine kids.

For a month I have been anticipating my first spring hike through the hills and hollers to see what is breaking ground. I know full well before ever setting eyes upon them that the Blue Cohosh is up amongst the Ramps (Wild Leeks) and Trout Lilies in the deep woods of Ramp Holler. The first spring beauty has bloomed and the Tooth Wort, an excellent wild edible, is budding. The Slippery Elms, Red and Silver Maples have all bloomed and will be producing seed soon. I see many deer and turkey throughout the woodlands this day. Lightning bugs are coming out from behind the layers of tree bark, and our earliest butterfly to show itself, the Morning Cloak, is flitting about the woodland in search of a mate's scent. On the forest floor last Fall's buckeyes and acorns have broken through their casings and their roots, spear-like, have entered the earth.

Around my yard I have missed most of the Crocus flowering—they can burst forth in an early warm spell of February—but the Daffodils have started their sunny yellow parade, helping to light up my home site.

The Lilacs are budded, just waiting for that first week-long warm spell to open. Ah, the Nettles—so much can be said about this miraculous giving plant—they're six inches high! Along with Chickweed, Cress, and Slippery Elm seeds, Nettles are a part of my spring diet. I steam or sauté them with onions, garlic, and sweet potatoes from last year's gardens. Nettles also form a major part of my daily tea SMANG (pronounced smangy)—Slippery Elm powder, Mint, Alfalfa, Nettles, and Ginger—which seems to help with my joint wear and tear while providing key nutrition. Nettles comprise 50% of this formula.

The red-purple tops of Valerian, and purple of Virginia Blue Bells, are poking up in the herb beds, giving some early color. The merry yellow wheels of Coltsfoot flowers dot the roadsides. Today is sunny and 65°, but this is only temporary in the March dance of extremes. Possible snow and cold rain are predicted for next week. This is a much colder spring than last year, which is not necessarily a bad thing. Flowering cycles are slowed down, and that might translate to more fruit. But in this region, late frosts after a warm, flower-stimulating spring can kill many of our fruit trees' flowers.

I would never have to grow a garden or enter a store, this land holds such bounty. I envision myself returning to the life of hunter-gatherer. Is it still possible? What would I have to give up? To me, true upward mobility is a return to simple living on the earth.

The years have cushioned the shock of just how much work needs to be done in spring—it all cries out "NOW!" Boxes of mail and packages and tens of thousands of lady bugs that have moved into my old farmhouse are waiting for me. Phone calls to answer and an article to write, but it's the first days of spring and my reflexes tell mc to sort out all of my garden seeds and sow a salad mix in the greenhouse. De-sprout the potatoes for planting. Check the bees. Haul manure. There are tools that need sharpening, and tires to fix, and tinctures to make, and more woods to visit.

March is my Guru! I have unofficially given March the title of "The Month of Moon in Flat Tire." It never fails that at some point in March everything breaks down. Have you ever noticed how if one oil tanker goes down another is soon to follow? I need to haul manure, but the small dump truck won't start, and it's not the battery. So I put some taller sideboards on the pickup to get on a bigger load, and the extra pressure breaks the tailgate, and then the four wheel drive goes out in the field. No big deal, I'll go get the big diesel tractor. Ah, but it is The Month of Moon in Flat Tire, and the tractor refuses to start. What next? Do I tell my friends who have come to live in this area about this phenomenon? I hear Chip and Amy had a rabid raccoon in their yard yesterday. Up at Willow Farm, they are pouring motor oil into their master cylinder, and Hank is playing bumper cars in his own driveway. Watch out boys, it's only mid-month, and the Guru is awake.

Soon, they too will understand that this is nothing but an opportunity for growth, non-attachment, flexibility, an examination of how vehicles can run our lives, and how to remain calm and anger-free because it's all small stuff anyway. In reality we are so blessed. I will never starve because I have Slippery Elm, Nettles, deer, and a forest of 10,000 products. It is spring, the earth is reborn, and we can all take part in something greater than ourselves. It is so beautiful here—the earth is awakening, the spring peepers are singing. The neighborhood I live in is filled with friends working, and dearly loving this earthly life. We can all laugh and help each other through this Month of Moon in Flat Tire.

Silver Maple unfolds from its winged seed case,
with Marsea's blonde strand curled around it.
That's a cow's tooth behind the sprout.

Photo Paul Strauss 1978

—3—
Leaving Apache Junction

This story takes place before I was ever in Ohio. I was 18 or 19 years old. I already knew I wanted to be an herbalist, farmer, and as self-sufficient as possible, and I was always trying to move myself toward those ends. I had been to the Woodstock festival, an incredible communal experience. I had already done enough to know that I was never going to handle society the way other people do. My father knew I could never live the way he expected and we had some tough years before his passing. I would tell him now that I am much wiser and I am sorry for my part. He was an incredibly brave man and I could only see things from my own narrow angle then.

I had spent time working in an insane asylum, on a locked psychotic ward, which gave me an incredible insight into societal pressures. I had access to the records and many of these patients had crumbled beneath society's pressures and their parent's demands. Some of these guys were on the ward for 20 or 30 years. Basically, back then, all therapy was drug therapy. Several times a day the nurses would come onto the locked ward, in and out, in and out with all the drugs. Rewards for getting guys to sweep or to do anything was cigarettes. We were responsible for shaving them because many of them were suicidal and could not be trusted with razor blades. One of the hardest parts of my job was wheeling the most suicidal patients to electric shock therapy. I must admit that this was not an easy thing to do and even today I have pictures in my head of the way they shook and their bodies bounced as the electricity was applied. After I wheeled them back it might be days before they could function at all again. Even today electric shock therapy is used with the most suicidal of people and those with psychotic delirium. It is done differently now, with a pre-sedative given and low voltage over a period of time. It is 80% effective for those who have no other options, and a miracle to many. This was at Boston State Hospital, just outside of Boston. It was a great experience for me overall. A state hospital where I could take the little electric train right there in the morning, and walk through a huge cemetery—one of those beautiful cemeteries, gorgeous places, old ones with big, old trees and interesting stones to read.

But that was another time. Now, in Apache Junction, Arizona, I was looking for something to test myself, to see what kind of skills I had. At the time, I had just come from a trip to many different Western reservations. The most recent one I had come from was the Hopi lands, where I learned about one of the signature plants I use now. The Hopi medicine man described it to me as the plant God gave them for everything. This plant is Chaparral, but many call it Greasewood. As you go west, at anywhere from 1,000 to 3,000 feet, you can see thousands of acres of Chaparral. It's got allelopathic toxins, and is all interconnected by the roots. Aspen trees are also interconnected; there are many plants that share this feature, as well as certain fungi. Some think Chaparral might be one of the oldest and largest living plants on the planet.

The Chaparral is widely used by all Southwestern Indians. I was a disciple of Chaparral and I wrote up literature and handed it out with bags of Chaparral I had gathered and dried—I was just trying to turn the world onto this plant. I was excited about a plant I believed in. The University of Utah had been having some success with it as a treatment for skin cancer.

I had some friends I was traveling with at the time; there were six of us and a couple of dogs. The dogs were big enough that each could carry a pack with their own food supply. I proposed that we should try spending some time in the historic Superstition Mountains wilderness area near Apache Junction, Arizona. They all said, "Yeah, we're in." I was the only one in the group with some skills for a prolonged wilderness stay, but my friends were all willing to try camping and hiking in this totally new environment.

The first thing we figured we had to do was go talk to the Forest Service in Apache Junction, look at the entrances, get topographic trail maps, and see what the hell we needed. Unbeknownst to us, the day we drove out of Tempe to Apache Junction there was a gathering called Indian Days about to take place.

Here was a kid—a group of kids—who were totally enamored and eager to learn more about native cultures. To arrive in Apache Junction on Indian Days was great timing. The whole scene had a colorful character, with a fair and festivities going on. We went to the Forest Service for a permit, and they thought we were crazy. There were millions of rattlesnakes coming out of hibernation. So the Rangers suggested we carry anti-venoms shots. We had to tell them our proposed routes and time of stay.

They said, "How are you going to eat? How are you going to live for such a long time in the desert?" I didn't see that as a big problem—I said we could supplement our supplies by eating rattlesnake. Their concern was that there's no way six people with limited skills and two dogs can carry enough on their backs for a month in the desert unless they harvested everything from the land. They were right, they saw the possibility of us getting into trouble. There were creeks running but no fish in them. When they told us this information we were disheartened because we really wanted to do this trip and stay in the desert for at least a month. This is a wilderness area…there are no vehicles allowed. There were gold mines and people going in and out with pack trains of mules or donkeys bringing in their mining supplies. Now it's a quiet, fascinating place that wears visible history. It is the fabled land of the Apache and the Lost Dutchman's gold mine that people are still looking for.

But what I saw in 1970 was different from what you see now. Today, large tracts of the surrounding area have been developed, there are golf courses and hotels. It's really built up, but still has that imposing stark skyline of the Superstition Wilderness looming right above the desert town.

So, my friends and I are enjoying our time at Indian Days, we're buying native food, purchasing Jasper and Turquoise, local herbs, and sweet grass braids, and then we hear an announcement that the final event of the day is the Burro Race. We decide we've got to go see this. Just outside of town is a grandstand where the race will start at around three or four in the afternoon. When we got there the grandstands were packed with thousands of people. We could see this event was extremely important to the people of Apache Junction and it looked like fun.

The way the burro race worked was that the Forest Service captured twenty or so wild burros. In order to gentle them a little they kept the burros in a large corral where they hold and halter break them and get them briefly accustomed to people. Apparently, after about a week, they can put a halter on them—not a bridle, a halter. They then bring them to the race site where the burros are enclosed in a small rope corral. The race is comprised of two stages: contestants first have to pick a number out of a big cowboy hat, then go to the starting line and at the shot of the first gun race off to find their burro and clip the lead line onto the halter and get the burro back to the starting line. The second stage of the race starts there, but this first stage was a big part of the fun.

So there we are. With the burros milling and shambling about, it looked intriguing, not to mention real dusty. There are a few black burros, but most were of the Jesus-type of burro, gray with black lines making a cross across their withers and back.

The whole scene was exciting. We're smelling the ever present dust but also beer and popcorn. You could see people all around us drinking, eating, shouting, and laughing, amped to be there. With all of the contestants gathered at the starting line, the announcer says, "Well folks, we have too many burros and not enough runners. Is there anyone in the stands..."

Before he even finished his statement I've already jumped up and shouted, "Yeah!!" and started down from my grandstand seat.

I'm there, excited...absolutely there, glad to have the opportunity to be a participant and not just a spectator. Right away, just like in Meigs County years later, people knew I was there. It was obvious that I was different in so many ways from the other contestants. I aspired to be more native than white. I had a bandana on my head and a ponytail down my back, holes in my jeans, and a great pair of broke-in Adidas sneakers, my moccasins, white with green stripes. Adidas had just come out before I left Boston and these were holy shoes to me. I felt like I could do anything in the right pair of sneakers. Ever have that feeling? The right pair...

My biorhythms must have been at an all time high that day. I was amped and in peak physical shape. Young and strong. I could see right away a lot of people snickering *look at the freaking hippie going down there, this ought to be good*. What struck me was that most of the native folks were wearing new Wrangler blue jeans, shiny big belt buckles and cowboy hats and boots—I'd never thought that local Indians would take this western culture to heart. But there you go. The contestants were half white ranchers, half native, and then myself, a New York freak more interested in the Indian world than the white world with which I was totally disillusioned.

Everyone I was burro racing against had cowboy boots on but I had on my trusty Adidas. I'm in there with the other contestants and the Rangers bring around a cowboy hat and everyone reaches in and picks out a number. I pick out mine—and it's the very number I wore when I played high school football, number 24! Well, that's pretty cool. I was struck with confidence by this luck of the draw.

We get to the starting line and, BOOM! The gun goes off and everybody has to run into the pack of wild burros to find their own. I was the first one in there by ten yards and had my lucky number 24, but you could hardly see in the thick choking dust. Once in the pack, you have to fend off burros with your hands, forearms, and elbows, pushing your way through. You definitely didn't want to fall down. Breathing was difficult, all these contestants scuffling around in their cowboy boots, also pushing the animals in search for their numbered burro. I find my burro pretty quickly, but others are also finding theirs. What have I got for him? I'm thinking…I need to make a friend; I need to make a good connection here.

In my left pocket I have Chaparral, the herb that I just discovered and was learning to use and love. In my right pocket is my pocketknife. I feel naked without a pocketknife. If I don't have it on me, I'm going to need it. This is still true today. But with the knife I also have Piñon nuts. One of the foods you'd want in the desert is this native nut. We were trying to find a source for fifty pounds of Piñon nuts to take into the desert wilderness as part of our food supply.

I also had a few peyote buttons. One of my fellow travelers was a member of the Native American church and he had five pounds of dried buttons and we were going into the desert to experience it fully. Not with high doses, but with small ones to open our hearts and minds to this ecosystem we had never experienced.

So I'm there at the start and I'm looking at my burro—you want to offer something when you meet someone. I pull out the Chaparral and the burro is interested, wiggling his nose, this plant is certainly part of his ecosystem but nothing he wanted to eat. I'm aware of the movement going on all around me. All this grunting, dust, and commotion, but I was in this world of my own, taking it all in. But the burro doesn't want the Chaparral.

I dig into my back pocket and pull out a dried peyote button, but he definitely doesn't want that either. I don't know if you've ever tasted peyote—could be up there as one of the worst tastes in the world. He didn't want it. I understood that.

Ahh, the Piñon nuts! I pulled a few nuts from my pocket, and this, my burro, a desert burro, knew and loved. He cleaned out those nuts in a flash so I made sure I had enough in my pocket. I had a plan, knowing that the way to an animal's heart and mind is through their stomach. I knew right away that my burro would follow me to the ends of the earth if I kept giving him Piñon nuts throughout the race. I got closer to my burro, scratched behind his ear and easily clipped my lead rope on him because what he really wanted was my nuts. I let him smell my hand again. Like dogs, equines are very smell-oriented—they're always smelling each other and smelling you. They're smelling everything. It's really wonderful how much information animals can get using their sense of smell. I notice that some of the other contestants have got their burros clipped and are trying to lead them. Many burros are pulling in the opposite direction. Some contestants were not willing to let go, falling down and tumbling in the dirt. Cowboy boot heels were being pulled off, and a few contestants were being dragged as their burros tried to escape. Out of maybe twenty-five people, only about fifteen could get a burro to the starting line.

Now we're on the starting line and the crowd is up and loud, really raucous. You have to race past the grandstand, about a half-mile out into a desert track, and then back around. And it's timed—whoever does the most laps in twenty minutes wins the race.

These guys, right away, they're all looking at me because I'm way different. This is good for me. I like that. Being different makes me feel really strong. It's good. I'm looking back at them and I've got a shit-eating grin on, smirking at them, you know, giving them the peace sign and BOOM! The gun goes off again. At least five contestants are going backwards at the sound. These guys are desperately holding on but the burros are taking them off into the desert in the wrong direction, dust marking their exit, and with rope burned hands they finally let go. The Forest Service was going to have to re-capture the burros to get the halters and lead ropes off because it's not safe for any wild animal to have lead ropes dangling.

We take off and, of course, I'm out in front just because it was my day and that pissed the crowd off. As a matter of fact, as we passed the grandstand the first time, I was probably already five or ten yards ahead. I had a burro that would do anything for me. Honcho, that is what I named him. As we go past the grandstand, the crowd is booing loudly—I mean, there were town heroes out here, and I was certainly not one.

But again, the booing made it better for me. Oh, now I have something to prove! I felt at that point, this might be my day. It's my day!! By the time I came around to the grandstand the second time, it was obvious that I was going to lap everybody two or three times. It was the burro's day, too. I slowed down by the grandstand this time and the burro just stopped, wanting some Piñon nuts out of my pocket. The burro is nibbling out of my pocket, eating out of my hands. I wave to the stands, put the Piñon nuts away, and we bolt out of there again. Half as many boos now. About fifteen minutes into it, the race is won and I'm just lapping everybody, so I figure, hmm…I'm really going to play this one up.

When we pull in front of the grandstand, I drop the lead rope and sit down. Then I lay down on my back. I take Piñon nuts out of my pocket for the burro, but it is the crowd that is eating out of my hand. Everybody likes me at that point because I am really playing the fool. Or not the fool. And then, we just streak back out there, run around the desert track some more, me and my Honcho.

I easily won the race, but didn't know until the finish that there was a cash prize. I won $300, which was a lot of money for a kid like me in 1970! But even better—I had won the burro! Honcho was mine to keep. And so, for $150 bucks I bought another burro, two pack saddles, and now we have everything we need for a long stay in the Superstition Wilderness area.

We were very well prepared but you just can't be ready for everything in the wilderness. On the first night making our campsite while clearing rocks for my tent, I turned over a stone and was immediately struck on my hand by four scorpions that had been living under the rock. I'd never been bitten by a scorpion before, but because I had done my homework about scorpions in Arizona, through the pain I remembered that the deadliest were the tiny brown gray ones. Fortunately, these were a much larger species. I was in pain and my hand swelled enormously. There was no ice or plantain available and the creek was a long ways away, therefore I just rode it out and by the next morning I still had some pain and swelling but was fine.

Next to watching my kid being born, the burro race at Apache Junction was probably the best day of my life. To walk up on such a scene as that in a totally foreign land, to be considered the enemy but then to exit to cheers and with our problem solved—what a day! A news photo of Honcho and I with Honcho's sponsor, the Apache Junction Drugstore, appeared in the local paper, the Gold Dust Gazette, the next day. I still have the canvas banner from Honcho's back from that photograph; it is now in the chicken coop thrown over the old Electrolux vacuum cleaner.

These memories make Apache Junction a holy place in my heart. It made me forever aware of the power of positive thinking, understanding that I could accomplish anything with the right attitude.

Working companions

Paul and Little Spot sharing a moment.
Photo courtesy Alana Galt-Theis

—4—
Meeting Bill

I'm writing to pass out what I call "The Green Spark"…I feel a responsibility to talk to people about plants and right livelihood, and how they affect people's lives and the planet. I come to this more fully through knowing my physical plane teacher, Bill Clonch.

This story happened six months before I met my farm. It was the first year I moved into Meigs County. It was the early fall of 1971. I was living with my girlfriend Laurie, who like me was originally from New York City. Laurie and I and another couple had been living up at an interesting place near Harrisonville in Meigs County; it was a Civil War era farm with bastard architecture. It was a big old place and we lived there for the summer rebuilding it with a friend. When the job ended we needed to find another place to live.

We met an older woman who said we could move into an old abandoned farm house on her land. All we had to do was fix it up and patch the walls. It had everything we needed. A two-seater outhouse. A clean well outside. There were four walls and a roof. We had to put a wood stove in the house for heat and found an old Hot Blast Florence stove with a mica view window that could burn wood or coal. We found a pitcher pump at the local hardware store and put it on the hand dug well. I love living simply. It's really no problem for me. I still live very simply. Simplicity is one of the keys to a good life.

We moved into the place and it felt good. I was twenty years old at the time. The place gave us access to an old garden site. It also had an old four-acre pasture that I could build fence around. I already had two riding horses and a milk cow. I hadn't gotten the mules yet, but the story is leading to the mules here.

We felt really happy being here. Laurie and I were both dog addicts and I'm still a dog addict to this day. I have probably spent more time with dogs than people…more time with plants than people, for sure. I have

Bill Clonch plowing with his team.
Notice the green ball cap.
Photo Paul Strauss

lived mostly by myself for thirty years of my life. I'm very comfortable in that place, especially since I live with all my animal friends and have access to so much forest acreage, an incredible community, and huge tracts of unused land and all its resources. It's a great situation.

We just had a beautiful litter of Wolf-Huskie puppies. At that time, I had long hair and obviously the neighborhood knew I was extremely different. In 1971, it was not easy having long-hair in Appalachian Ohio but I never minded that. For me, I derived power from being unlike the norm, and found it gave me the opportunity to talk about what I believed in, especially plants.

The third day after we moved in, we went to town. There was a Kroger grocery store at the time in Pomeroy, right on the Ohio River. When we came back from town, the whole litter of our beautiful innocent puppies had been shot on our front porch; blood was everywhere, the mother beside herself, a horrible scene to come home to. It was a warning, obviously. It was very hard to accept. To this day I have that image burnt in my heart. As you must know, puppies are a joy of life. We always kept our puppies for nine or ten weeks just to be around them longer before we sold or traded them. To find that scene was heart-stopping. "What the fuck?"

We buried the puppies. Yet even though it sat heavy on our minds, we went ahead with our lives, fixing things up, doing, but always knowing that most people just did not like us. That's just the way too many people are though. If they don't understand something, if someone's different, they don't like it. Somehow it's threatening. And hate is easier than compassion and understanding.

The following morning, I decided to take my heavy heart for a walk down Heisel Run Road. It was a fine late spring day, clear and bright right down to the horizon, warmth already in the air, with only the highest of cirrus clouds. Walking down the road I remember hearing something jangling, clanking, and the sound of a great deep voice. That is when I came upon one of the most beautiful sights I had ever seen. It was my future physical plane teacher, Bill Clonch, plowing his big bottom field with a large team of mules.

I grew up in New York City but had spent time around horses and rode often. I had always been comfortable with animals and I had envisioned living with horses when I got older and left home. Not only did I want to ride, I wanted to know how to work a team and be responsible for growing my own food.

Walking up the road and coming upon Bill plowing with a team of mules temporarily took my mind off my problems. I just stood by the corner post and gave witness to this spectacular scene. Bill was a big, strong, impressive man in his prime. He grew up in a family of 13 kids, all born at home. His family never had a car. He and his father were giant people. The whole family was almost totally self-sufficient, which is what I wanted for my life. I wanted to at least have the tools to be self-sufficient, to be responsible for as much of my being as possible and for my animals also.

Bill was a bright and cagey guy and he must have known somebody was there standing by the corner post watching him. He was able to take in a lot. Anybody who lives and works in the woods knows you have to be aware of your surroundings. You have to use your peripheral vision and interpret the sounds of the forest. It's been a life-long quest for me to do that as a means to understand my ecosystem. I just stood there mesmerized, very quiet. When I get quiet, I get the big ear, sound becomes an important tool for me. I'm watching this guy plow. He's "Geeing and Hawing" his team through the field. Gee is right. Haw is left. I'm noticing that every time he comes around to the end of the field when turning the team around, one mule drops into the open furrow. I see right away that's how he was keeping his rows straight.

I was so into it, I kind of left my body. I was just watching this go on and when you do that, things become extremely evident. I could hear the metallic clanking of the traces, those are the leather lines hooked to the collar that become the chains attached to the single tree or double trees that pull the plow or disk. You hear the sound of roots popping as the earth turns over, the heavy breath of the horses, the smell of their sweat. The deep tone of Bill's commanding voice filled my ears. The focused attention it took to do this task was inspiring. I was just so into it and must have been watching Bill for about fifteen or twenty minutes. I believe Bill knew I was there and what I was thinking, knew that I was appreciating his work. I know he knew who I was because everybody knew hippies were now living down the road.

Bill must have made about four or five passes, before he turned around and brought the team to a halt so the mules' heads were right next to mine. For a minute, he didn't say anything. That was kind of cool. Being so close now I was aware of the smell of the horses' sweat and the sound of their deep breathing, watching their chests heave in and out, and the way Bill easily laid the plow over like he'd done it a thousand times. I felt I was in a different world, and I was. Bill took his dirty green ball cap and turned it to the right, still saying nothing, reached inside his left shirt pocket, and took out a pack of Camel cigarettes. Right away I see he's got nicotine stains on his fingers. I worked at a mental institution so I know nicotine stains on people. He smoked three packs of Camels a day. He pulls out a cigarette, lights it up, takes a drag, exhales, and the first thing he says to me is, "God, you must be one of those god damn hippies moved in down the road."

The way he said that, I instantly knew I was being embraced and not threatened. I also knew that he was not a person who hated me because I was different. As a matter of fact, this guy was interested in me, which was kind of rare during that first year I was in Meigs County.

I was taken aback and stuttered, "Yeah. I've been watching you for a while and I always wanted to learn how to use a team." He'd already seen my horses down the road tied up in an old flowerbed that morning, so he knew I had some equine interest.

Then he said, "I heard your dogs were shot on your front porch. News travels fast."

The only thing I could mutter was "Yeah. That sucked." Bill responded with "Yeah. I think I know who did it. Tell you what, Paul, why don't you and your friends come up to the house tonight at six o'clock and Battle Axe will make you some dinner. Six o'clock. You be there." For Bill, Battle Axe was a term of affection he used to refer to his wife Retha. She called him her Stud Muffin. I also knew that when he called her Battle Axe it was not derogatory. He wasn't talking her down…this is a guy who dropped out of school four days into the sixth grade, basically because the teacher told him he couldn't miss any more school days doing farm work, and to stop smoking in class. He said "to hell with you" and walked out. That was the last day he was in school. A few days later, at twelve years old, he was working in the coal mines with a team of ponies because they could get them in the strip holes.

That was the most exciting thing that happened to me in weeks. I meet this amazing guy. I still didn't know he was going to be a teacher, but I just flew down the road to tell my friends. I met this guy Bill Clonch and he's got a big team of work mules. I was probably salivating and sputtering with excitement. He wants us to come up to meet Retha, his wife, he calls her Battle Axe and she's going to make us dinner. We've got to be there at six o'clock sharp.

It was powerfully refreshing to meet a local person who was interested in us. We finished our work in the garden, put on a clean pair of clothes and the four of us went walking down the road.

As we're walking, I was towards the middle of the road, my friends on the side. I hear a pick-up truck coming up behind us and slowing down. I'm wondering, is this a good thing? The truck slows down and stops right next to me, and the guy in the passenger seat sticks a knife right out of the window, uncomfortably close to my throat and says, "We just killed your damn dogs and I'm going to cut your damn hair off." Quite a day. I was startled but not scared. I had just spent almost a solid year in the streets of Boston being attacked by police and being thrown in jail for protesting the illegal Vietnam War. I was young, fast and strong and knew there was no way he could touch me. I whispered to my friends, "Walk on, get Bill, I'm going to deal with this idiot." I saw if he opened the door I would have kicked it shut on his arm. Let's put it this way, it wasn't a gun. It could have been a worse situation.

Nowadays it might have been a gun. Basically, I was saying really stupid stuff like, "Why do you hate us? I'm a nice guy. I'm going to put a big garden in." I was trying to make my case but he just hated me. He hated all of us. He hated the world. My friends were freaked out. They knew where Bill's house was and ran breathlessly up the driveway. Bill is like me. If he's supposed to be someplace at six, he's ten or twenty minutes early. Bill was on his porch waiting and my friends rushed up shouting,

"Paul is in trouble. There's a guy with a knife on him. You got to help."

Bill gets in his red Dodge pickup. Doesn't say anything to my friends. He's all business. This is a call to action. Bill is probably happy this is going on because he already didn't like this guy. From this point on it could have been a great movie scene.

Here Bill comes driving real fast down the driveway, I can hear him spitting gravel. I'm in the middle of the road, a good step back from the knife, but not far enough back that I couldn't have put my foot to the guy's door if he decided to come out. All of a sudden Bill is on the other side of me. I look at Bill, I smile, feeling good, my new friend is here. He's obviously a lot bigger and stronger than anybody around. He's probably forty at the time. I'm between heaven and hell. I look at Bill and say, "These guys are the guys who just killed my puppies and they're going to cut my hair off." Bill looks at me for one second. Says nothing. Classic. He turns his head sideways and engages this guy's eyes. Just locks them up. This guy's in trouble, I can see the knife slowly being withdrawn. Bill still doesn't say anything. I'm looking at Bill with a questioning face, what is going on?

He takes his hat, I see he moves it to the left. Once you get to know Bill and he turns his hat to the right, it's all good. If he turns his hat to the left, you want to get the hell out of there. He's not having a good day. Bill turns his hat to the left. Doesn't say anything. Puts his hand in his left shirt pocket and takes out a Camel cigarette. Smokes two or three hits on the cigarette. He's not letting the son-of-a-bitch's eyes go. Without looking at me Bill says something very simple, "Well Paul, I tell you what we're going to do." He reaches down to the floorboard of his truck, "Here," he hands me a crowbar and says, "I've got a hammer and we're going to work on these bastards." This is now my day, I'm ready to go to work with my new friend. Bill opens the door to get out. I raise the crowbar and those guys just peel out and escape as fast as they can. In one second, without even really knowing me, Bill had protected me. It endeared me to him for the rest of our lives. They never bothered me again. As a matter of fact, twenty or so years later, they knew I was an herbalist and organic farmer and they had all kinds of questions for me. They made apologies for that day and the killing of our beautiful litter of puppies.

That's how I met Bill Clonch. He only said things when they were important. Here's a guy who understood self-sufficiency, who ended up teaching me how to use a chainsaw. Taught me how to work a team. Taught me so many skills in the woods, not just the names of trees but also how he used each species, how to manage the woods, make a living in the woods, how to shoe horses, fix a harness, build a drag sled, fix a barn. I had met my perfect physical plane teacher. Thinking back on those days, I believe as time went on a lot of local people in the 70s became interested in me because they could see my beautiful gardens and the rebuilding of my old farm and of course they associated people with long hair as knowing how to grow marijuana and wanted seeds.

At one time Bill had been a moonshiner. As a matter of fact, Bill told me about a farm that sat right next to his old home place that was for sale. He said there was a big cave on the property that we used to make moonshine in and you might be interested in this property, Paul. The minute he said there was a big cave on the property I bought it in my head without even looking at it. This is where I live now, it was 80 acres at the time and he just knew it was right for me.

Bill became the father I never had. I feel incredibly grateful to have experienced another father figure in my lifetime. Bill gave me the skills, the energy, and the attitude I needed to live this herbal farm life.

Bill and team taking a break.
Photo by Paul Strauss

Paul plowing the house garden with Jerry and Big Red, spring of 1979.
Photo courtesy Marsea Ilio

Paul and Jerry tilling the sweet corn
with a five-shovel cultivator.
Illustration by Wendy Minor Viny

Two Appalachian Species:
Black Locust & Bill Clonch

Bill Clonch was a big, hardworking, hard-headed man…exceptionally strong, but kind…strong-willed, but willing. Bill dropped out of school at the age of twelve when his teacher told him to put out his cigarette. Hell, he'd been working his team of mules for a logging outfit all year. Bill figured he didn't need school anyway, and he never gave up his habit of three packs of non-filtered Camels a day. Growing up on a subsistence farm with thirteen brothers and sisters, he could do about anything having to do with these Appalachian hills…doctor a horse, develop a spring, build fences, raise a barn, dig Ginseng and Goldenseal, make moonshine, farm, garden, hunt, butcher, and provide. Bill had been a father, farmer, miner, horse trader, logger, coal miner, and construction worker. He had those Marlboro Man good looks even when all of his teeth were gone. But the feature most people remember was the irrepressible twinkle in his steel blue eyes set inside this rock of a man.

1971 was my first year on the farm, which fortuitously sat next to Bill's old home place, and saw my start at rebuilding the original 80 acres I had just bought. I began by rebuilding the farmhouse and barns that were built around 1870, while at the same time clearing pasture, building fence for my stock (two riding horses, a work mule, and a milk cow) and rebuilding rundown soil with only a shovel, single mule and a drag-sled. At the time, I could purchase 100 tons of turkey manure for $100. I was young and poor with my work laid out before me. I can clearly recall the deep green stripes of pasture created by the reawakening of dormant, undernourished legumes and grasses. To satisfy my need for fencing, building materials, and cash, I started a fence post business with Bill and the mules. We cut from the tens of thousands of Black Locust trees that graced the farm's hillsides. Once a week, we had a customer that would buy three hundred seven-foot line posts, and fifty gate and corner posts. We got fifty cents for the seven footers, and a dollar for the nine footers. We didn't lack for work.

The Black Locust is one of the most useful trees on any farm. Posts set two and a half feet in the ground thirty years ago are still in good shape today. Being strong and rot-resistant, Locust is a superior material for cabins and decks, and makes super-hot firewood that can be easily split. The posts last even longer when split with wedges. I remember one large tree, although half dead, gave us seventy posts. The first years on the farm we had healthy three-foot-diameter Locust trees. Some of their stumps still stand.

Locust is leguminous, soil-nourishing, and casts a beautiful shade. In spring, the blooms are spectacular, laden with cascading bundles of creamy white flowers. Their sweet fragrance drifts for weeks over surrounding hills, adding to nature's spring symphony. Honeybees maul the blooms, and in years of heavy flow, I was able to extract hundreds of pounds of its light-colored honey. These same blooms are wonderful treats when frittered.

Locust starts easily by seed, and sprouts from its own roots. A pioneer species, Black Locust can take over pasture and hay fields left un-mowed, and is certainly as valuable as cattle in many cases. Forty-foot shade trees now stand fifteen inches in diameter from the stumps of my original cuts. Locust, along with Tulip Poplar *(Liriodedron tulipifera)* are excellent permaculture trees. The beans may be used as emergency food, and farm animals love its foliage—nibbling lips move easily around its thorns. Bill remembers having to cut down large quantities of Black Locust to keep his stock alive during a terrible drought in the 1930's.

As I revisit this in 2007, although there is still a high population of Locust, the species has been highly degraded in the last thirty-five years. The culprit is not only the Locust Borer, but also the Locust Leaf Miner, browning and skeletonizing the leaves by the end of July. It is now difficult to find good Locust in the area. There are stands of healthy Black Locust left in West Virginia, Virginia, and New York, and some pockets of Ohio. I think one reason is a combination of the trees being the subspecies Shipmast Locust, and lower bug populations. It seems that isolated Black Locusts in forest settings are not getting as much bug damage as those on the edges of our forest where their numbers are higher. This is a pioneer species, always moving into old farmland where higher populations attract more bugs.

Botanists know our local Locust as Black Locust, or *Robinia pseudoacacia,* which has such a sweet sound. Bill was aware, as I am now, of white and yellow varieties lumped under the same scientific name (one being flesh-colored when cut, and one a deep burnt-yellow). The yellow variety yields a far more durable wood than the white, and it seems more impervious to the locust borer. I have also heard of a sub-species of *Robinia pseudoacacia,* called the Shipmast Locust, famed for its strength and durability. Maybe the Yellow Locust that I know is this variety. Taxonomy, while useful, can sometimes lead us in circles.

After cutting the trees to size, we would make piles on the hillsides of ten to twenty posts, and chain them together with a self-tightening dog collar-like chain that Bill called a snaking chain. Working with our mules—me with Jerry, and Bill with Big Red—we'd snake the piles out of the brush and down the hill to a landing that sat above the road. The mules got so good that, once we were out of the woods and on a cleared trail, we could drop the lines and tell the mules to get up. They would bring the load down the hill to the pile, stop, and wait to be unhooked. Then we'd head back up the hill to do it again. The trip was roughly two hundred yards. There were places on the high ridges we could take a steel-wheeled wagon pulled by the mules. We would pack the posts uphill, and load the wagon with about fifty posts. The wagon was built specifically for posts, or small logs. It had no bed, and the posts lay easily between the bolsters, locked down tight with binder and chains.

Locust is best cut when the sap is down. On a beautiful late fall day, on a high hill, Bill and I were riding on top of a fully-loaded wagon. I asked him how to slow a heavily loaded wagon while going down some of our steep hills. I knew this was something Bill had to do every summer because many of the best hay and cornfields were between the highest hills. Bringing the crops down from the upper fields to the barns and stock was part of an endless summer ritual. Hauling manure back to spread on the fields completed the loop.

> Farmers—the gears circling between the cycles
> As seeds swell in the spring rain.

"Ah, I'll show you how to do it," said Bill. He stopped the mules and rough locked the rear wheels with a chain so that they wouldn't turn. It seemed reasonable, and back up on the load we went with Bill heading the team straight over the hill on a slope of around forty degrees, with fifty-five posts and two of us on board. At first it seemed that everything was okay, even on this steep-ass hill, but halfway down, I sensed that we were in deep shit. Little did we know that fall's leaf litter had balled up under the wagon wheels, making an uncontrollable sled of the entire rig.

I can still see Bill fighting to hold the team back. Two massive animals digging in, rear legs to forelegs, straining to hold back the heavy load of posts. It was impossible. The mules were in big trouble and Bill, knowing that we were out of control, threw the reins and shouted, "Jump!" Each of us went flying in opposite directions. Somewhere between soaring through space and somersaulting through the brush, there was a loud and sharp crack, almost like a shotgun blast. After checking on each other, we discovered that the wagon tongue had broken from the pressure and had driven itself three feet into the earth, stopping the wagon and literally saving the mules' asses. "Damn good thing that tongue wasn't made out of Locust!" Bill cried. The poor mules were shaking, totally lathered in sweat, wild fear in their eyes, but okay. We unhooked them, pulled off their bridles, cooled and watered them, and tied them in the shade.

Now, Bill and I had to face unloading the disabled wagon on a steep hillside. With the wagon in a twist, the chain tension was so great that we couldn't release the binders. Never one to wait around, Bill grabbed a double-bladed ax, and with one massive Viking stroke, cut the chain in two. The sudden release of tension sent the spring-loaded binder recoiling toward Bill, busting him above the eye, and knocking him to the ground. I madly chewed up plantain and forced it into the wound of my blood-soaked friend. A minute or two later, Bill came to and waited for the bleeding to slow. Then he sat up with a Cheshire cat grin, lit a Camel, and got right back to work as if nothing happened. I remember him muttering how he had brought the wrong ax, how he would have been fine if he had brought the long-handled ax he normally carried. We unloaded the posts and went up to get them the next day after fixing the wagon.

Looking back, I understand how Locust and Bill have much the same personalities…giving, strong, useful, and thorny. Gratefully, I realize how my life has been enriched to have known these two Appalachian species.

Bill Clonch, Paul, Laurie Leshin, Retha Clonch
1971

—6—
The Cave of the Fallen Cow

If you have read any of the previous stories about some of Bill's and my adventures, you can see that when Bill was young his family was pretty much self sufficient. They lived simply and grew or hunted for the majority of the family's food, and also grew most of the feed for their animals' needs. They were big people of Scots-Irish decent. While Bill lived at home his family never owned a car. Bill told me often that if both teams were working and they had run out of oats for the horses, his dad would walk the four miles to Langsville and walk back home with a hundred pound sack of oats over each of his shoulders. No big deal.

Bill's mother was knowledgeable in the use of local herbs and had mid-wifery skills. There were thirteen kids, all born at home, and Bill was somewhere in the middle. He was a kid who wanted to learn his dad's formidable earth skills.

In today's terms, it was more like an Amish upbringing. If you didn't do your chores, you didn't eat. The belt was not spared if you really dis-obeyed. I can understand it, everybody—no matter how young—had to pull their share for the support of the family. Fast food did not exist, they had no bank account, no money to borrow. A telephone and elec-tricity came much later. They dug their own coal and cut their own wood for heat,—chainsaws also arrived much later. Wood was cut with a two-man saw and split with an axe, a sludge and wedges. There was no TV, only radio on some evenings. Work was sun up to sun down with a break for part of Sundays. Most of the time they had no refriger-ator and food was eaten fresh or home canned. Meat was also canned or put into salt barrels. They hand dug their wells and the springs they needed for water. An outhouse was the bathroom for everybody and there was a line every morning. Every year they would fill the hole, dig a new one, and move the outhouse over it. Good idea.

So once I'd gotten to know him well, Bill told me about this cave. He knew I wanted to buy a piece of property and told me about a nearby farm that sat right next to his old home place, the old Charlie Amos place on McCumber Hill Road. It was 80 acres with an old farm house and barns from the late 1860s or early 1870s, and it was for sale. Bill thought all the buildings could be repaired slowly, but every one needed attention.

Oh, and the farm has a big cave on it, he said, big enough for many horses and cattle to get some shelter in the winter. It served as a moonshining cave at one time and had also housed an escaped convict from the Lucasville penitentiary for a year and a half in the early 1920s. An old box spring he had dragged down there is still there, rusting away. To live in a cave through an entire winter the man had to have some formidable outdoor skills, but late the second spring he got desperate and was caught stealing the neighbors chickens and was sent back to jail.

On top of the cave is a spring that creates giant icicles 40 to 60 feet tall around the mouth of the cave. Bill had helped farm most of this place for much of his young life and therefore knew all of its secrets. Just the thought and excitement and history of the cave made me realize I wanted to buy it even before seeing the farm. Bill also told me that for hundreds of years before his family got there it was used as a campsite by the Indians who traveled through these fertile hills on their hunting parties. He had often found arrowheads whole and broken playing in the cave as a child. It was so exciting to me as a young man. I could feel my future calling.

It took awhile for Bill to tell me the story about how the cow fell over the cave. Bill's family often farmed the 17 acre field above the cave. Now, there is a pond I built there, with Poplar woods surrounding it. I have also built a solar powered cabin by the pond and have let this pretty Poplar wood grow up since I have been here, and these trees are growing fast and straight in the rich soil (You can read about this amazing species in the tree section).

In the fall after the crops had been gathered—usually alfalfa and corn grown in rotation—they let their stock in to glean the field. After the animals were grained in the morning and the cow milked they were turned out to wander back to the field for the day. In the evening Bill's dad would shout "SEBOYS!" real loud a few times and they would all return to the barn by themselves for their evening feed and milking like clockwork. The feed was a basic mix of cracked corn and oats with molasses. Sounds pretty good, I could eat that for my breakfast hot cereal. Besides a team of work ponies and a big team of draft horses, their family milk cow, Molly, was a vital part of their subsistence life, especially with so many children. Bill says it seemed for awhile that as soon as a baby came off his mom's breast another one was ready to take its place.

An abundant milk supply helped make it all possible. Back then, the milk was never pasteurized, just placed in the spring house to be kept cool after it was run through a simple funnel milk filter. All of the kids drank milk. Every day the cream would slowly rise, and from it fresh butter was churned. Part of the milk was allowed to clabber to make fresh cottage cheese every other day, which was eaten with salt and pepper, or put on hot corn bread with butter, or mixed into soup beans. To keep a cow milking she must be kept pregnant—calves were used for meat or raised and taken to market. Any extra milk was fed to the hogs and chickens. Nothing was ever wasted. The big treat for the kids was fresh-made ice cream, maybe a couple times in a good summer. Bill remembered how good it was draped in berries or peaches from their farm on a hot summer evening.

At nine or ten years old Bill was helping with all aspects of the farm including milking Molly, to whom he became very attached. One evening after the first hard frost in late October all the stock came in except Molly. They knew something was wrong because no animal will miss their chance for sweet feed and it was also time for her evening milking. Bill and his dad headed out to the field to find their missing cow. Bill was eleven or twelve at the time. About halfway there they heard her loud bawling and knew Molly was in trouble. They hurried on faster. As father and son came around the corner and got a view of the big cave their hearts sank. They could see she had fallen off the lip of the cave and had missed the big rock, but was splayed out in the shallow water below the cave. She had busted her leg and probably her hip. She was in horrible pain and could not get up. It was amazing that she was alive.

The way it happened is this, in my reckoning. In my time on this farm I've lived around a lot of big animals and there are always the dominant ones that control the food and water. Molly was likely drinking from the spring and got pushed out of the way, slipped on the new ice and slid over the lip of the cave.

Bill and his dad were standing on the steep hill just above the big Basswoods when they saw Molly's predicament. Back then the Basswoods were eight feet in diameter. That whole cave holler was virgin timber, it had never been cut. It was all cut in 1957. Today, a whorl of six trees has sprouted from the original stump.

Bill described to me what a devastating scene it was for them. Molly's pain and bawling was amplified as it bounced off the cave rocks. She was struggling desperately to find a way to get up, but it was impossible. Bill and his dad ran down the hill as fast as possible to be by her side. Bill was a man-child, at twelve he was probably bigger than I am now. His father was 6'4", broad and farm tough. That was the kind of man Bill was growing up with. Bill never lost that image. He always had a need to be seen as strong, tough, resilient, and highly skilled. It eventually ended up killing him at too young an age.

I often try to imagine what it must have been like for father and son to stand next to Molly in her great pain, trying to figure out how to help, fighting their emotions. She was a crucial member of their family. Bill's dad made the decision I have had to make five or six times in my life, as any farmer has to make, when faced with a mortally wounded animal. Death is natural and inevitable, but pain and suffering have to be dealt with mercifully and quickly, as your only job in that moment. I have had to put down a beautiful quarter horse colt whose joyous life filled me with joy. He had broken his leg in two places riotously running through our hillside pastures like any young foal does. And there were the dogs I loved, who were hit by cars on our country road by drunks. I can remember my confused mind, trying to hold it together, to get the gun and load it as my hand and heart shake violently. I felt Bill's pain in that moment. I know I have never lost mine. Those times are locked away in the tight corners of my brain that I choose not to visit often. But this tragic responsibility is part of accepting a farm life.

Bill's dad takes him by the shoulder and looks him deep in the eyes. He says, "You know Bill, she's our Molly. I know how much you love her and milk her every day, but she can't stay in this pain. I'm going to stay here with her, you run and get the .22, not the shotgun, as fast as you can."

Bill scrambles up the hill. He told me that he was in tears that he did not want his dad to see. The guy never cried. He said his dad could whip him and he never cried. But he was so attached to Molly. The thought of her in all this pain got to him, and he cried at the thought of losing her.

Bill gets back to the house and the family keeps asking, "What's wrong?" He really can't talk but sputters while in motion, "Molly's hurt and I have to get the 22." He goes into the house to get the gun, but then realizes that he can't do it. That's it, he just can't shoot his Molly. So he puts the gun down and goes back outside. He hooks up the team of big draft horses to the drag sled, and also grabs a rope. The drag sled with its Black Locust runners is a far better choice to get down into a steep rocky holler than a wagon with wheels. The drag sled is small, low to the ground, and more stable than a wagon because of the runners' friction on the steep hills—the runners can grab and slow the descent.

Bill brings the team and drag sled around to the cave and when his dad sees him he is furious. "Bill I'm going to whip your ass, I told you to bring the 22!" Bill says to his dad, "I just couldn't do it dad, just couldn't do it. I brought some rope though."

So his dad knows now that they just have to deal with the situation.

He's stuck with it. The kid brought the drag sled, there is no gun. We deal with it.

He calls up to Bill, "You work that team down that hill! You work it by yourself!" So this twelve-year-old kid works the team slowly down that steep, rocky, twisting slope. When he reaches the bottom he works the drag sled around and positions it beside Molly. He pulls off the sideboard.

So now Bill and his father, man and man-child, roll their bawling thousand-pound cow onto the sled and secure her with the rope. It had to be a loud and difficult task with Molly in so much pain. But to get her out of the holler would be no easy task for any team. Bill told me it took over an hour just to get her up to the trail. The workhorses had to be incredibly strong to bring that drag sled and a thousand-pound animal against gravity, up that hill and over rocks. But they got Molly out of there. Bill's dad was trying to be stalwart and carry on, but was also real angry when they got back to the barn.

In most barns there are regular-sized stalls and one or two big box stalls where you might keep a stallion or a mare or heifer about to have a calf. They were able to pull the team and sled to the open box stall door, then roll Molly in.

Maybe you have never milked a cow, but it is essential to milk twice a day, morning and evening. If you do not, the cow can get the lymphatic infection Mastitis. The same infection can be a problem for any human mother. So now Bill had the difficult task of milking Molly while she lay on her side on the ground, which isn't easy, believe me. But he did it twice every day. Because you are on the ground, there is no room for the milk bucket, so Bill milked into a smaller quart can that was then poured into the bucket, back and forth till Molly was milked out.

I think of these stories and the life these people led, and it's just remarkable to me. It's why it's so nice having an Amish population around here now, living a non-technological life. I just love it, as did Bill. It makes perfect sense to me. The world is now being eaten up by its own advancements and pollution, and the earth is suffering.

To finish the story though, another animal most farm families had was a beagle. Beagles fit in perfectly with a self sufficient life. They have an incredible sense of smell and are used to hunt rabbits. The way it works is that the hunter has a shotgun loaded with small No. 6 shot. You send your beagle off to do what they know and love to do. When your dog picks up the track of the rabbit, he starts baying real loud while running it. Even though the hunter can't see his dog, he can track it by the incessant barking. A good dog will bring a rabbit around in a circle close enough for a hunter to make the shot and provide dinner. Beagles are amazing work animals in that way, and another mainstay animal on the farm.

So Bill's family always kept beagle dogs. At the time, they had a summer litter with a runt in it. He was the weakest one and became a pet to the family, even though he irritated the other dogs and was not real good at hunting. About two months after they set Molly in the box stall—two months laying down on her side—this runt beagle jumps a rabbit out of the house garden and starts running it. The rabbit sprints around the barn with the runt in hot pursuit. The second time around the barn the rabbit darts into Molly's box stall, the beagle follows, coming in fast and loud, and in that perfect instant Molly freaks out and jumps up. She jumps up and stays up. Back on her feet, she lives for a good time longer and even manages to walk, although with a severe limp, for the rest of her days.

So in the end, Bill made the right choice as a twelve-year-old kid. That's why, when I bought the land, I named it The Cave of the Fallen Cow. It's not just the story, it's the ideals of a life led close to the bone. Just how tough and skillful these people were and what these young kids had to see, what they had to deal with, and how they had to grow up so young. Bill told me that he remembered that by age five he was given chores to do every day. The next year it would be a harder chore. That's the way these families survived.

Ramp harvest (wild Leeks) in
Ramp Holler, early spring

Time to switch pastures
Illustration by Wendy Minor Viny

7

Indian Summer 2003

O ne of the strongest glues holding me to this particular piece of land is the gift of Indian Summer, which I affectionately call the second flowering.

Our hills burn with color in early fall. Days are warm, humidity is low, the clouds are high, a sky of mare's tails. The air is alive. Unlike last fall, in a year of little color, deer death, and much cold, this fall seems endless and dreamy. We were blessed with three gracious rounds of bliss, each one ending with a few days of cold and rain that surely must signify the end. But then, wham, here are a few more weeks of mild autumn weather to revel in. Work is so enjoyable these weeks—time seems to slow as you glide through fall's farm tasks. You could give me any heaven on Earth this time of year, high mountains or balmy beach, and this is where I'd choose to be.

Fall is the time to dig roots and make cider. This year, through mid-November, I have red raspberries every day, the gardens are still full of kale, beets, chard, mustard, lettuce, parsley, arugula, and cilantro, all made tastier by the cool nights. Apples are in abundance—the king of all fruits with so many varieties, usable in so many different ways. With friends, we juice three quarters of a pickup load and make sixty-four gallons of cider to put up. I have been using the same hand-crank apple press for thirty-eight years—it was used in a local orchard over a hundred years ago. Juggling mugs of fresh cider, watching out for the ever-present yellow jackets, we apple dance around each other, laughing as we take turns at the different tasks of the juice job. Shoveling the apples into the shredder. Cranking the shredder and its hundred-pound flywheel. Turning the auger press and its 3-inch diameter screw. Waterfalls of apple juice fill small pots to be moved into big pots and then to be poured into gallon jugs for freezing. This is not work but a warm flow, a frenzy of friends leading a good and bountiful life. Replace the pickup with a horse and wagon, and it could have been two-hundred years ago.

To top it off, one of the things that comes together this fall is the first production from an apple orchard I planted seven years previous that will replace the first orchard I planted after buying the farm. What a treat to taste the new varieties! Every apple is Christmas-morning good after such a long and expectant wait.

This year also sees the absolution of guilt from a recurring twenty-five-year-old idea that this will be the fall to make a huge planting of Ginseng in the forest. With the help of other botanically-obsessed planting fools, we put in over ten pounds of Ohio ecotype seed in over a hundred acres of forest. That's a lot of plants and a lot of possibilities, leading to next spring's forest game of finding the baby sang. On my calendar notes, I call it the re-ginsengization of the farm. The future is calling.

Part-II
—The Big Herbs—

Illustration by Wendy Minor Viny

White Ash
Fraxinus americana
Oleaceae – Olive Family

Unfortunately, there is a good chance that our stately and plentiful Ash trees may go the way of the American Chestnut and Elm. White Ash comprises up to 20% of total stands of tree species in these forests; it is now a pawn in the game of international trade that brought the Emerald Ash Borer from China. The forest service has pretty much given up hope for the survival of the White Ash. It is another of our forest treasures that may be heading for its demise. It will be sorely missed by all who appreciate its gifts and beauty. My great hope is that we can find a way to protect and preserve this tree, each one a treasure, for both the forest ecology and for future plant lovers, and all those other life forms that depend upon it. I hear that most of the Ash trees in Michigan are dead, and in Cincinnati the Ash is being slaughtered by the borer.

White Ash is our largest Ash species. It was named White Ash because of the whitish color on the underside of its leaflets. There is also some Green Ash on the farm and Sanctuary in good ground. Compared to White Oak, Ash is fast-growing and easily sprouts from its stump when cut. It is late to leaf out in spring and in late summer and fall has winged seeds or 'keys' on the female trees—these look much like canoe paddles and stay attached to the tree late into fall. Young green keys were used as a food source by native people. In fall, the White Ash can assume a variety of colors, from luscious gold to rich purple to bronze with mauve highlights. Its bark is distinguished by deep diamond-shaped furrows on mature trees.

One of our most utilitarian woods, White Ash is renowned as a hot-burning firewood that has the ability to burn either dry or green because of its flammable sap. Straight growing with a beautiful wood grain, it is highly prized in floors, furniture, and cabinets. Strong and pliant, its wood is prized for Major League Baseball bats, hockey sticks, diving boards, oars, as well as for shovel, hoe, and pitchfork handles.

Once as a young man I was clearing pasture in the late fall near a dry creek bed. I remember there was a hard frost that morning. As I cut about two-thirds of the way through the trunk of a medium-sized, unhealthy Ash tree, it shuddered and literally jumped ten feet away from its stump across the creek bed as if it were spring loaded. It was the only time I have ever seen this happen. A hundred years ago Ash was used by some as barn door latches because of its ability to spring back and forth without cracking, splitting, or losing its strength. Ash is one of the main trees in whose leaf litter I hunt for the tasty morel mushroom in early spring, and in whose dying wood I find the medicinal mushroom *Ganaderma applanatum* or Artist Conch.

We are lucky enough on my farm and the Sanctuary to have high numbers of mature Ash trees. There is one with a four-foot diameter that overlooks Golden Healing Pond, the first pond I built. I met her on my first day at the farm forty-five years ago—her canopy shades a quarter-acre. Many of our White Ash trees have two- to three-foot diameters—"Centenarians"—but I had to log out many older ones toppled by the July 1999 tornadic down-draft event. Together with members of our intern program, we turned these into the lumber used to build Tornado Cabin on the site where many once stood.

I am constantly trying to figure out my forest management plan when I see trees dying wholesale. It takes about two years for a tree to die once the Emerald Ash Borer moves in. I struggle to process this—these trees in our vast forests cannot be saved, what should I do? How many should I harvest? I believe it is an honor to their lives to do something useful and creative with their bodies that have given so much to our ecosystem. I am well aware that their death will provide nourishing topsoil for the forest, but I will also turn some of these dying trees into lumber. It seems that time may be fast approaching. I am not looking forward to it, but I will be a part of it. Change is our constant.

Big Toothed Aspen
Populus grandentata
Willow Family

I hope you have experienced the splendor of the Rocky Mountain's signature autumn tree, *Populus tremuloides,* the Quaking or Trembling Aspen. Our Southeastern variety, the Big-Toothed Aspen, is similar but has more of a smoky-grey bark color and is paler than its beautiful sister. Because of its long, flattened leaf petioles, its leaves also dance or "quake" on the slightest breeze. It is a short-lived, fast-growing tree that prefers well-drained, sandy soils. It may be found upland or near streams.

Its buds and catkins are eaten by many birds. Deer browse the buds, bark and leaves. Its soft wood is harvested for use as a paper pulp.

Our Big-Toothed Aspen grows to be a much larger tree than the Quaking Aspen. In these forests, it can be upwards of 70 feet high with a long, clear trunk. Fall coloration is a softer yellow, unlike the glory and vibrancy of Quaking Aspen's translucent gold.

Along with Locust, Red Maple, and Virginia Pine, Big Toothed Aspen is a species that has naturally reclaimed many strip mines in this area. Aspen can also quickly reclaim areas after forest fires because its roots sprout easily and quickly. It can serve as a nurse tree under which more valuable and long-lived hardwoods may become established. Its spring flowering is profuse. If you travel along the paths of the Big-Toothed Aspens in the spring, you may be lucky enough to run into the sight of clouds of its billowing downy seeds blowing away from its mother's catkins. An awesome sight!

Big-Toothed Aspen's wood is weak and breaks easily in storms. After the 2003 President's Day ice storm, I had to reopen trails through large swaths of its fallen trunks. Aspen is also one of the beaver's favorite foods and building materials for its dams and homes.

Basswood
Tilia americana
American Linden, Bee Tree
Basswood Family

We have some Basswoods on the property, but there would have been so many more a hundred years ago. At one time, Basswood greatly outnumbered all of our other hardwood species. Although now not as populous as Ash, Oak or Hickory, this fast-growing species is a tree well worth knowing. If left alone, it is a stately spreading tree that can have great girth and height.

Basswood's large heart-shaped, saw-toothed leaves have prominent veins. By mid-summer the tree casts a cooling and dense shade. In June and July its creamy white flowers are clustered on pale green wing like blades which turn into nutlet-looking seeds. Their flight goes on throughout the winter. Cut trees will readily sprout back. Propagation is easy from cutting and seed. Below the big cave (the Cave of the Fallen Cow) stand two old-growth, seven-foot-diameter basswoods cut in 1957. Each stump now has a whorl of trunks 70 feet tall shading stands of Trillium, Blue Cohosh, Black Cohosh, and Ginseng. Life goes on.

Its leaves, a faded yellow in autumn, are often marred by wind and insects and drop early in the season helping to create the rich soil in which it flourishes. Twigs of Basswood are loved by deer. The buds and young emerging leaves have been used by First Nation people for food. An infusion of its flowers has long been used as a remedy for nervousness, indigestion, and coughs. Along with Chamomile, it is a long-recognized European tea often used after meals or before bedtime. The Basswood flowers profusely and creates a 'humming tree' as bees gather large quantities of its nectar, which makes a wonderful gourmet honey. The inner bark, or bast, is a food source that can be harvested from younger trees. On older ones it is tough and fibrous and was widely used as cordage, for clothes, and for fish nets. The soft white wood of Basswood is very light—America's balsa wood—and has been used for fruit baskets, toys, model making, bowls, and carving.

Basswood was, at one time, the most populous tree species in the virgin forest of the Ohio River valley. But because of its usefulness, its numbers have been drastically reduced. A stately, interesting, and highly medicinal tree, it should be considered for planting today in our forests, farms and backyards. It's also a lovely tree to plant in cities and towns for its land-scaping value. Many choose to plant the European Basswood, which is a much smaller tree and an easier one from which to gather flowers.

Beech
Fagus grandifolia
Fagaceae

T he American Beech is one of the most widely-distributed trees in our country. A forest aristocrat, it is one of the most useful and beautiful trees in any forest.

It is the sole representative of its genus in North America. On the Sanctuary we are lucky to have an abundance of them. One section along the medicine trail is known as the "Beech Woods" due to the concentration of mature Beech trees growing there. But many of these older ones are now in demise.

Throughout the seasons, this tree is one of the easiest to identify because of its trunk's smooth, cylindrical, silver-grey, granite-like column. The smooth bark is a survival mechanism left over from its tropical days—smooth bark is harder for vines to get a hold on and climb up.

Beech leaves are bright and beautiful, a glossy green 3-5" long with sharp teeth. In the fall, the leaves turn a soft golden yellow. If the year has had any moisture, standing under a large Beech in autumn is like being in a golden chapel of light. I look for these trees in October; they never cease to render me instantly religious—quiet and thankful to be here now.

Beech leaves can remain on the tree into the winter, and on younger trees last all winter. The brown buds are unusually long, very thin, and pointed. A slow-growing tree, Beech does best in rich, moist loamy soils, sometimes forming almost pure stands. All First Nation people who lived near beech forests valued its small, sweet nuts as a food source, going so far as to search out chipmunks' winter stashes. Of course, it's also a major food for squirrels, birds, turkey, deer, and fox. Farmers would turn out their hogs to fatten on Beech nuts and Oaks' acorns. Birds do much to plant the trees, but these seedling trees are not so numerous or vital as the sapling growth that sprouts from the roots of parent trees.

Though now extinct, the passenger pigeon was at one time so numerous in this country that they were said to blacken the sky. Their fall migrations were fuelled by Beech nuts. Farmers would kill pigeons by the thousands to fatten their hogs.

John James Audubon, the French-American ornithologist, naturalist, and painter, was also a wonderful writer. He wrote a vivid account of the mass arrival of passenger pigeons in a Beech forest on the Ohio River in Kentucky. There were so many that their numbers broke limbs—hundreds died entangled in branches that fell to the forest floor. In his illustration of two courting passenger pigeons depicted in the fall, you can sense his longing for his wife, Lucy.

Because of the disappearance of our vast Beech forest and the mass slaughter of the passenger pigeons, the most populous animal on the face of the earth was driven to extinction. There are still centenarian Beeches in our forest, four-plus feet in diameter and 80 feet tall. Because of their tendency to become hollow, Beeches were never cut for timber. Beech is the condo of our forest, providing a home for raccoons, squirrels, birds, and bees. Not bad—having a home that can also be your food source. Beech is also an indicator of rich and limey soil, and they were cut en masse to increase our good farming ground.

An interesting plant associated with the Beech trees is the Beech Drop, which attaches itself to the host's roots. The Beech Drop has no need for the making of chlorophyll like other plants, as it lives off its host but does not seem to harm it.

Beech Drop

Beech wood is tough and has many uses. One of the most interesting is its use for clothespins. It makes a wonderful fuel when seasoned, but rots quickly when left on the ground. It has also been used for tool handles, flooring and furniture, ice cream beaters, and other kitchen tools. Many authors, including Bryant, Thoreau, Tennyson, Virgil, and Shakespeare, have written about this magnificent species—I think you'll appreciate why once you stand beneath its 'golden bowers' in the fall. Bryant wrote of the Beeches in England, "the groves were God's first temples." Then Thoreau, "no tree has so fair bole, and so handsome an instep." And then there is the frontier writing cut into an old Tennessee Beech tree:

D. Boone
Cilled A Bar
On Tree
In Year 1760

Sweet Birch
Betula lenta
Cherry Birch or Black Birch
Birch Family

The Sweet Birch common in our area prefers to make its home in deep, rich, moist, well-drained soils. I find many in the hollows of our beautiful Hocking Hills. Even though the healthiest and largest trees are in the hollers, I also find some on the upper trails, in rockier soil and rock outcroppings. This species grows throughout the Appalachians and as far north as southern Maine, where it is more populous than its southern relatives in Georgia.

The two most identifying characteristics of this tree are its wonderful, spicy aroma when twigs are broken, and the taste of wintergreen in its twigs and leaves. Its bark is dark and a shiny mahogany-red when young, and develops into deeply-furrowed and broken large irregular plates with age. The bark is not papery, like most Birches, and this species is often confused with Black Cherry, which is why one of its names is Cherry Birch.

Its leaf can be from 2.5-6 inches long, 1.5-3 inches wide, and is broadest near its base with serrated edges, and pointed at its tip. It turns a bright, clear yellow late in the fall. The flowers, both male and female, are catkins, and the males are larger. (A catkin is a spike of unisexual, apetalous flowers with scaly, usually deciduous bracts.) Sweet Birch fruits are erect cones

1-1.5 inches long. Its tiny winged seeds are sowed by the wind when ripe. Songbirds feed on its seed—grouse eat the seed and also the catkin. Deer browse the twigs and young leaves.

Sweet Birch's wood makes for hot-burning firewood. Because its wood is so hard to season and warps easily, it has only been cut seriously into lumber with the advent of kilns. Like our better known Black Cherry, Cherry Birch's hardwood deepens in color with time and air, and has been sold as "Mountain Mahogany." Sweet Birch has the same chemical makeup as the small understory herb Wintergreen, and until recently it is where all of our wintergreen oil came from. Now Wintergreen oils are produced synthetically from salicylic acid and alcohol. This oil has a market in flavoring candies, gum, and drugs. I know of its use for joint pain.

Our First Nations people knew how to make Sweet Birch into a food by shredding the inner bark and drying it in the spring when it is rich in starch and sugar. These shreds, like spaghetti, were boiled with fish to make a nourishing dish. I have for years heard about Birch beer and now know how it's made. Sweet Birch can be tapped in the same manner and time of year as our Sugar Maples; corn is added as a fermenting agent and then filtered out when done. Anyone need a new project?

Black Haw
Viburnum prunifolium, Caprifoliaceae
American Sloe

Black Haw is one of our beautiful understory shrubs. It can grow in many different soil types and locations. I have found it in our woodlands, on stream banks, on hillsides, and in unfarmed clearings. Attractive clusters of white flowers adorn it in spring, and in autumn it puts out small, dark blue to almost black, edible berries. These half-inch-long berries get sweeter as they hang longer into fall, and I often enjoy them as a nibble. The edible outside encases a single flat seed. Large amounts of these fruits can be gathered and, with a little concentrated effort, a small family could put up a lot of Black Haw sweet fruit leather. Later in winter, turkey, quail, grouse, and a variety of songbirds and mammals eat the fruit. Deer browse the young twigs and leaves.

Black Haw leaves are opposite, and as its species *prunifolium* implies, these leaves look similar to Plums and Cherries. Easy to spot, the small serrated foliage has a red tinge that is a flag to my eyes in a woodland setting. Its branching is short and crooked, and the trunk has a checkered bark while the branch bark is smooth.

I have planted Black Haw in my arboretum as an ornamental that I also eat and use to make medicine. Black Haw is not as popular in plantings as its close relative Nanny Berry *(Viburnum lentago),* also native to our area. Also worth mentioning, we have much Maple Leaf Viburnum *(Viburnum acerfolium)* in our woodlands; it is a smaller understory plant whose exceptionally soft leaves turn a beautiful pink in the fall.

Black Haw has long been used medicinally by our First Nation people, in a similar way as Cramp Bark *(Viburnum opulus).* The part of the plant used is the root bark, usually gathered in the fall after the leaves have fallen. This bark should be tinctured immediately or dried in the shade so it does not lose its properties. It is a uterine relaxant used for uterine cramping and false labor pains—and a classic herbal treatment for threatened miscarriage. It may also be used as an anti-spasmodic for asthma. Its sedative and relaxing properties have been used to lower blood pressure.

Ethnobotanists and historians write of Black Haw's use as one of the first instances of biological warfare in the United States. King's American Dispensatory of 1854 states, "It was customary for planters (slave owners) to compel female slaves to drink an infusion of Black Haw daily to prevent self-abortion by taking cotton root bark." Cotton Root induces abortion for unwanted pregnancies. Need I say more?

Yellow Buckeye

Aesculus octandra

Hippocastanaceae - Horsechestnut Family

Sweet Buckeye – Big Buckeye

The Sanctuary property has many mature Yellow Buckeyes. Most people who visit for classes or hikes have never seen this wonderful tree, and are immediately enchanted by it.

There are mature Yellow Buckeyes on our north-facing Medicine Trail, near Hydrastis Heaven. Yellow Buckeye is noted for being one of the earliest trees to leaf out in the spring of the year, and one of the earliest to drop its leaves in the fall. The showy, stacked, upright yellow white flowers appear when the leaves are half-grown. Our ruby-throated hummingbirds feed on them as some of their first available food sources upon their arrival in the spring of each year.

Yellow Buckeye is a large-sized tree. The bark is ashen grey, and broken into thick scaly plates. I often associate it with alligator skin. Nothing else in our woods has this look.

Buckeyes require good soil and drainage. Leaf buds are large and noticeable all winter; they open in early spring, before Oak and Ash even break their buds, to become large attractive five-fingered leaves. The large shiny seed is toxic and is rarely eaten by animals. The only reference I have found is to Fox Squirrels eating these seeds. When the seed capsules split open, they partially expose the large shiny seed, which looks like the half opened eye of a deer—hence the name "buckeye."

Our First Nation people knew of its toxic properties and threw crushed seeds into ponds, stunning fish for harvest. They also knew how to leach out these poisons and make the nut edible.

Yellow Buckeye is the softest and weakest of our hardwoods. It's been used in the manufacture of boxes, paper pulp, and most noticeably, artificial limbs. The tea or salve has been long used for piles or rheumatism. Closely related to Horse Chestnut, it has similar properties for use in varicose veins.

Yellow Buckeye is similar to the Ohio Buckeye, *Aesculus globra,* our state tree and the symbol of Ohio State's powerful football team.

Butternut
Juglans cinerea
Walnut Family
White Walnut

Butternut is related to Black Walnut and wants the same rich, moist, well-drained soil. Bottomland, creek, river valley, or rich hillside will do it just fine—in these conditions it can make fast growth. But it is a rare find these days in most places; the disease Butternut Dieback, also known as Walnut Canker, has killed most wild trees of this species.

Butternut is shorter than Black Walnut, and relatively short-lived. Like Black Walnut, Butternut produces aleopathic chemicals that keep some plants at bay. But the nut is good forage to all species that appreciate Black Walnut. The nuts are more egg-shaped and pointed at the tip, and the shell is deeply furrowed. The kernel is oily and sweet, but only when young; I prefer them to Black Walnuts. The green husks are uncomfortable to handle; they're fuzzy and clammy to the touch, but sticky at the same time. No amount of washing will get the dark stain off your hands. This dye was much-used during the Civil War. Wearing Butternut dyed jeans, southern backwoods regiments were called Butternuts.

Young trees are ashen grey, developing broad flat ridges that are not as deep or dark as mature Black Walnuts. Like Walnut, it is late to leaf out in spring, and early to lose its leaves in autumn.

Being a very light and soft wood, it is easily worked and was used in fine cabinetry. Its finished wood is lustrous and satiny, never warping or cracking. It was much sought-after for interior paneling and altars in the 18th and 19th centuries.

There is a small grove of Butternut trees at the Sanctuary. We clear brush around them every spring to ensure they get enough light. They share a rich fertile site with such woodland herbs as the Green Dragon and the rare *Passiflora lutea*.

Small doses of tea from the root bark or the inner bark of the trunk was a favorite early American laxative. Crushed nuts could poison fish and bring them to the surface. Iroquois used the nut oil for cooking and as a hair dressing. The sweet sap could also be boiled down into syrup.

Butternut is another once-common tree that has all but disappeared now, along with the American Chestnut, many Elms and Dogwoods, and soon possibly our Ash trees. This is all happening in a relatively short time. What will be left? Get planting and protect those remaining. Trees are among our most valuable resources.

Eastern Red Cedar
Juniperus virginiana
The Pine Family
Red Aromatic Cedar

O ur Eastern Red Cedar is a handsome, small to medium-sized tree, usually cone-shaped. Red Cedar is the most widespread conifer in Eastern North America. It is slow-growing and quite drought-resistant. Around our area it prefers to grow on dry, well-drained soil with a limestone underlayment. In such areas it can form large communities. At the Sanctuary, you can see this on the hill just to the north of the greenhouse—twenty years ago, there were very few Cedars there.

Cedar's deep-green leaves are scaly and sit opposite one another. Broad at the base, they taper to a point. The leaves are resinous and have an aromatic smell. Their small fruits are glob-shaped, berry-like cones and are also resinous. Dark green when young, they turn blue at maturity.

Cedar's bark is thin, stringy, and reddish-brown in color. It has red aromatic heartwood that is very lightweight, brittle, and weak. The predominate smell of a cedar is from the oil.

Cedar wood takes a good finish and is used for interior trim and sills. It is made into chests to protect blankets and wool clothing from moth infestations. Cedar closets are often built into homes, to protect clothing from bugs. The house I grew up in, now seventy-five years old, has a built-in cedar closet in the basement. I loved its smell before I knew the tree. At one time Cedar was the primary wood for wooden pencils. Now, most of the largest trees have been cut.

The Incense Cedar, *Calocedrus decurrens,* is now used for pencils. Red Cedar makes a long-lasting fence post. Forty-plus years ago, I cut a standing dead Cedar and set it as a corner post in my first pasture fence. Then, twenty years ago, when changing my pasture system, I dug it up. It was still solid. So I set it again as a corner post 3ft. deep in a garden fence. It is still sound today and may outlast me.

Cedar makes long-lasting outdoor furniture and shingles and was used in boat building. I love its hot-burning, good-smelling kindling. And I just paneled a small solar outhouse with its aromatic wood.

Since the demise of our wild honey bee populations, carpenter bee populations have soared and are boring into Red Cedar's soft wood for their nesting sites. This makes it no longer fit for any outdoor use around here. And I see this same carpenter bee in Hawaii.

The ranges of the Red Cedar and the Robin Redbreast are the same. The Red Robin dearly loves the Red Cedar's seeds, and have become the tree's main planters. The gorgeous Cedar Wax-Wing, as its name implies, also uses Cedar as a primary food source. They also love Poke Berries. The American poet Robert Lowell, a keen observer of nature, tells us that before heading southward:

> The sobered Robin,
> Hunger-silent now
> Seeks Cedar berries blue,
> His autumn cheer.

Cedar berries are beloved by game birds such as quail, grouse, pheasant, and turkey. Cedars make a secure hiding place in which birds can nest. Cedar is an uncomfortable tree if you like to walk barefoot in your yard.

It carries the fungal disease Cedar Apple Rust that looks like a yellow gelatinous alien. On apple trees, these spores infect the leaves with damaging yellow blotches. When Cedar is overtopped by an advancing forest, they die, but the wood can still be used—dead-standing or down, it can remain untouched by rot for a long time.

First Nation people living near Red Cedar used the berry tea for coughs, colds, and sore throats. It induces sweating; the smoke from its leaves was inhaled in rituals for purification. I often place it wet on steam bath rocks, or make a tea of its leaves to pour over the hot rocks and inhale its fragrant, healing steam.

Most people in America know this tree and recognize its warm, aromatic scent, and have at some time come in contact with its wood or oil.

Down the road at Ralph's property, through an Oak wood atop a steep hill, sits the oldest cemetery in the neighborhood. Around its perimeter stand Red Cedars, now 175 years old. This cemetery holds the grave of a Revolutionary War Soldier and many small stones marking the graves of children who died in the 1918 Spanish Flu Epidemic. Cedars are revered as helpers of spirits ascending to heaven. I often see them planted in old cemeteries, along with Periwinkle and Yucca.

Black or Wild Cherry
Prunus serotina
Roseacea Family

T he wild Black Cherry (or "Wild Cherry") is one of the easier trees to identify. With its dark reddish-brown rough bark, 'broken' into irregular scaly plates that curl at their edges, it stands out. Cherry does best in moist, well-drained, and fertile conditions, where it can become a large tree.

Wild Cherry foliage is toxic to humans and livestock, containing prussic and hydrocyanic acid. These acids give the tree a bitter almond flavor. Farmers fear their cattle being sickened by eating its fallen dried foliage, and so tend to clear Wild Cherry trees out of pastureland. Farmers clearing their pastures have given me plenty of Cherry trees to log out, which I've worked into beautiful lumber.

I have some Black Cherry growing in my pastures and have never had a problem—I even noticed that the mules and donkey have nibbled at its bark with no ill effects.

In late spring, when its leaves are almost fully grown, the Cherry's white drooping flowers appear. In August the fruit is purple-black, very shiny, and about the size of small peas. It's much-desired food for most birds and mammals in our area, who help spread the species and its germination process by running the seed through their digestive tracks.

The great defoliator of our Cherry trees is the Eastern Tent Caterpillar, which forms webbed tents in the forks of the trees. Heavy outbreaks occur cyclically, for two to three-year runs, at approximate ten-year intervals. Cold wet springs slow these cycles down. These destructive pests also get into my cultivated cherry, apple, and peach trees, and also my blueberries. I try to keep up by destroying their egg casings in early spring, tearing down their existing tents, and squashing the caterpillars. In branches too high to reach, I mount a propane torch on a pole and burn the suckers out. There are always plenty of caterpillars, and I can always use more fruit. Unfortunately, only a few bird species eat the tent caterpillar.

The Black Cherry is the only lumber tree in its genus. Its beauty is highly valued by furniture and cabinet makers, and much of its wood is cut into veneer. It is a very hard and close-grained wood with a unique reddish-brown color that takes a beautiful polish and darkens nicely with time. The demand for use of it in furniture and cabinet-making has been so great that Black Cherry is growing scarce and needs protected areas like this Sanctuary to thrive.

Pennsylvania has some of the largest reserves of healthy Black Cherry. In our forest, it is hard to find perfectly healthy Black Cherry because so many were injured in the 2003 President's Day ice storm.

The Black Cherry's aromatic inner bark has been used in herbal medicine as a tea and syrup for coughs, bronchitis, colds, and sore throats. This medicine can be obtained by pruning from branches. Never gather from the main trunk, and never girdle a tree.

Appalachian pioneers drank Cherry Bounce, a drink that mixed Brandy or Rum with a pressed juice of ripe Black Cherry fruits. As a child, I loved Ludens' Wild Cherry Cough Drops—like candy!

The unique look of the bark and the smell one gets by scratching the twigs makes this forest beauty easy to recognize. Wild Cherry is a wonderful shade and park tree, standing alone or in the company of other hardwoods.

Eastern Cottonwood
Populus deltoides
Willow Family

Though there are only a few on Sanctuary land, I include our Eastern Cottonwood because they are abundant elsewhere in our region in wet lowlands, near rivers, near streams, and in swamps.

This is an extremely fast-growing tree that can reach over a hundred feet in thirty years in the right conditions. Cottonwoods are asymmetrical with glossy foliage and, like all Poplars, the leaves respond to the lightest of breezes, dancing on their long petioles. The leaves are alternate and serrated, 3-7 inches long and 4-4½ inches wide. When Cottonwoods are young their bark is a smooth yellow gray, becoming dark gray and deeply furrowed as they age. Squirrels and beaver eat Cottonwood bark, leaves, and buds, and beavers use it to make their hutches. Deer feast on its tender twigs and foliage.

Our Eastern Cottonwood was brought West by pioneers onto the tree-less plains, where it now provides important shade along small streams and rivers.

Cottonwood is a very soft and weak wood that warps easily; it has some limited use for packaging material and light crates. Cottonwood is not a tree to have near home sites because its large, ever-reaching root systems find and clog drain pipes and sewer systems, and have the ability to raise and bust up concrete.

Most vital to understand are Cottonwood's long, pointed, resinous and fra-grant leaf buds. The resinous sticky material is Propolis, a gum resin that protects the unopened leaf. The Cottonwood gives us a way to easily har-vest this tremendous herbal remedy by gathering its early buds. Another species related to Cottonwood, *Populus balsamifera,* is the renowned "Balm of Gilead" of Biblical fame—another source of healing resins.

Propolis, Pollen & Honey

Propolis is one of the most potent of nature's natural medicines and is used in tinctures, salves, tablets, and capsules. I have relied on Propolis for years and can attest to its remarkable healing powers—it's a top-ten remedy, and I'm never without it. It is effective for a wide range of conditions includ-ing wounds, infections, ulcers, diarrhea, frost bite, strains, herpes sores, sun-burn, rheumatism, bed sores, coughs, most lung problems, hemorrhoids, and sore throats. It is strongly antibacterial and seems to stimulate healing wherever it is used. You can make a resinous bandage over wounds by just letting a few drops of strong Propolis tincture sit on a plate and thicken, then dabbing it on the wound area. Being a gum resin, it will stain and it is difficult to clean up. I'll spare you the gory details in the array of wounds I and my animals have sustained over our forty years on the farm, but will tell you that Propolis is one of the keys to their quick healing.

To beekeepers, Propolis is known as bee glue. Honeybees gather Propolis and bring it back to the hive in their pollen baskets. Due to its sticky nature, the bees must work cooperatively to help each other remove it (not true of pollen, which they can remove themselves). Although it does not kill mites or small hive borers, bee glue molds and seals out cold drafts and is used by bees as an antiseptic rag to clean out recently-hatched larval cells before the queen lays in them again. If a mouse gets into a hive, bees can sting it to death but have no way to remove the body; in that case, the bees totally embalm the dead mouse with Propolis, sealing in all contagion.

With my hive tool I clean Propolis off the top bars and hive tops where it is stored, and there are now Propolis traps available to make collection easier. But you can buy raw Propolis from beekeepers and its products are sold at most health food stores. I have always thought that one of the reasons my Immune Extract and Golden Healing Salve work so well is the large amount of Propolis in these formulas. I've found it to be rare, but some folks have sensitivity to Propolis and can experience a rash on application.

Pollen is another incredible substance gathered by bees and then collected by humans in pollen traps. Pollen has been called "the most concentrated, nutrient-rich food in the world." Homer refers to it as "the food of kings." Bees use this plant sperm, which is very rich in enzymes, vitamins, and minerals, as a source of protein to feed their developing larva. Pollen helps the body adapt to stress and fatigue, and stimulates the natural immune system. Pollen is used by people who are convalescing to help bring back their strength and by athletes for endurance. It is a supplement used in well-being diets, in smoothies, and for skin healing. It can also be used in flour when baking or as a wilderness flour itself, or as a direct wound dressing. But some people can have allergic reactions to some pollen and should not use it.

Much like the Cottonwood tree makes Propolis easily available, the common and abundant Cattail makes it easy for humans to gather pollen. When pollen is ready on Cattails, they'll show a fine yellow dust; take the heads and invert them into a small paper bag, then bang them around gently while holding the bag closed. It will amaze you how much pollen you can gather from a good-sized Cattail patch. The Apache consider pollen sacred, as do I.

Raw unheated honey is a remarkable burn and wound dressing. Big tanks of honey were made available to burn patients in England in World War II. Besides just using raw honey as a sweetening agent, there are so many ways to use all of the products the honeybees gather and make, like Beeswax. Not just for candles, Beeswax is the base for most healing salves and lip balm.

Flowering Dogwood
Cornus florida
Cornaceae

S mall and slow-growing, the Flowering Dogwood is considered an understory species throughout the Eastern United States. Most people notice this beauty in early spring when it lights up the woodlands and fields with its showy white flowers before its leaves appear. Technically these are not flowers, but bracts—tiny true flowers are clustered in the bracts' centers.

Again, in the fall, the Dogwood gets to show off with beautiful, bright red clusters of berries that remain on the tree for a while even after its red leaves drop. These oily berries are an important food source for birds. The combination of bright crimson berries and red fall leaves is known as foliar fruit flagging and is designed to attract birds which may excrete its seeds many miles from the original tree.

Dogwood bark is unique, having a checkered appearance which reminds some people of alligator skin.

Sadly, 75% of the dogwoods in this area are now dead or dying. The culprit is the anthracnose fungus. Trees on the edge of the woods or in fields are doing okay because of better air flow. It was not that long ago (ten or fifteen years) that throughout our extensive woodlands, the Dogwood's white bloom could be seen everywhere in spring. White explosions in a forest still mostly asleep, its green still a dream. Almost all of these Dogwoods, young and old, have died. My memory is always aware of this past beauty, a signpost of spring. I am always saddened by this recent loss. I am afraid that this is just the tip of the iceberg of species loss in our forest. "The times they are a changin'" (too quickly).

The hard, tough wood from this tree has been used for engraving blocks, and for tool handles. Implements designed for repetitive use and wear like the fingers of the cotton gin, shuttles of high powered industrial looms, and even golf club heads were made of Dogwood at one time. Small twigs were made into chewing sticks for dental health, and the inner bark was used for fevers and diarrhea, and to fight Malaria during the Civil War.

Dogwood's outstanding beauty has made it well known here. Introduced into Europe, it can now be found in many European gardens and parks. You can help this species through its tough times by planting a few in an open location. You will always be glad you did, and so will your children and birds.

American Elm
Ulmus Americana
Elm Family
White Elm

When I moved to the farm in 1971, next to the old silo foundation and small milking shed was the eight-foot stump of a dead American Elm. Its mighty trunk was in the creek, not quite rotted away yet. In a series of aerial photographs I obtained (the oldest one I estimate to be from 1938-1940) you can see the huge crown of this Elm shading the whole barnyard. There are many skeletons of large and small American Elms around the property. Luckily it is a prolific seeder that can start producing seeds at 18-20 years of age. A few larger remnant Elms still reside in our woodlands, but the days of the old Treaty Elms is over.

American Elm is one of our best known trees—its range is almost anywhere east of the Rocky Mountains. It is not particular about soil type and does well in varied situations. Before 1930 it was a favorite for street and park plantings in many U.S. cities. As America expanded westward, many settlements were built up next to a giant Elm. Unfortunately, in the fifty years after the arrival of Dutch Elm Disease, two hundred million trees succumbed. Before this time it was considered a hardy tree, its character being tall, graceful, and wide-spreading.

American Elm has a classic vase shape, usually with a weeping appearance. It has a gray-to-brown, roughly-furrowed bark, often with a green hue. Both its alternate leaves and disc-shaped seeds resemble those of Slippery Elm, but are smaller. American Elm leaves are 3-6 inches long, and its seeds are 1/3-1/2 inch long. The seeds are crucial food for birds, squirrels, and mice. Deer browse its buds and twigs, especially on younger trees.

When American Elm was plentiful it had myriad uses. Its yellowish-brown wood is soft and light, but very resistant to splitting due to its interlocking fibers. This is why it was so important in the manufacture of wagon wheel hubs. When it was plentiful it was also used for saddle trees, cheap furniture, boxes, and crates. The American Elm is not a good firewood and is certainly not worth the energy to split by hand.

A woodland that has had Elms upon it, or still has an Elm population, is a good place to hunt for the tasty morel mushroom in the spring. Around the farm, this is usually the second week of April, about the time the black snakes are coming out.

American Elm sapling bark was braided into cordage. In 1775, George Washington took command of the Continental Army under a large spreading Elm tree. Washington has another connection to Elms—his diary states that he was always looking for Elms to transplant to his farm at Mount Vernon.

Young American Elm is a good choice for building a sweat lodge or wikiup if Willow is not available. It has the ability to bend without breaking. With fewer American Elms around and Willows a half mile from the sweat site, I find my bamboo makes great lodges, the smaller canes being less likely to split than the big ones.

Interestingly, at one time American Elm was used in the construction of early automobile bodies. With its fibrous nature, it holds screws better than most other hardwoods and won't split easily. But it does not make a good lumber because of its tendency to warp easily.

Scientists have now developed Dutch Elm Disease-resistant hybrids, named Valley Forge, New Harmony, and Independence. These were cloned from resistant American Elms.

Slippery Elm
Ulmus fulva or *Ulmus rubra*

Plants rule! Without them, there would be no life as we know it on Earth. Plants are the only living things that produce oxygen, food, medicine, and untold numbers of other necessary products by eating dirt, air, sunlight, and water. Plants have no need for verbal communication, shoes, war, taxes, or short trips to the store. In many ways, I see them as a higher life-form. Self-sustaining, plants are environmentally safe and generate their own energy. Oh, what it must feel like as a plant is bathed in the first rays of morning's sunlight! "Plants," as Scooter Cheatham reminds us, "are the only organisms that make protoplasm, the very substance of all living cells from raw elements, the vital umbilical link that sustains all life."

One of my favorite plants is *Ulmas fulva,* commonly known as the Slippery Elm tree. It certainly demonstrates the sustaining nature of the plant kingdom. This amazing tree is on the top of my "ten most useful plants" list because I have seen it help so many. But unfortunately, it is in decline in much of its native habitat. Where I live, in the fertile foothills of the Appalachian Range, this is sadly evident. The culprit is a fungus, *Graphium ulmi,* commonly known as Dutch Elm Tree Disease. The carrier, the Elm Bark Beetle, arrived on North American shores in a boatload of logs from the Netherlands around 1930. Dutch Elm disease has affected not only Slippery Elm, but most other native Elms as well. Urbanization, logging practices, and mining also contribute to the ever-decreasing numbers of this remarkable giving tree.

Slippery Elm prefers rich soil and substantial rainfall, and can attain a height of 60 feet with a trunk diameter of up to 2 feet. The inner bark of the tree has long been valued for food and medicine, but given the increasingly at-risk nature of the species, its branches are used instead of the main trunk's inner bark. On the farm, I have found that I can use the inner bark of trees that have contracted the disease and will be dead in a year or so. The inner bark is mucilaginous with a sweet, earthly fragrance and flavor.

Slippery Elm flowers in the first delicious warmth of late March or early April, before its leaves appear. The greenish-brown seeds, larger than those of its sister tree the American Elm, also appear before the leaves. The larger leaf buds are visible through the plant dormancy, and are downy with red hairs. Both Slippery Elm and American Elm are dominant succession species, moving quickly into old pastures and hay fields along with Sassafras and Black Locust. Strong and beautifully grained, the wood of Slippery Elm is hard and reddish in color. I've been told by old-time woodsmen who grew up in this area that it is suitable for outdoor use.

In forest surrounding my farm, I am fortunate to still have some larger, older Slippery Elms that have not succumbed to the Dutch Elm Tree Blight. I fear this may be a short-lived situation and that these trees may go the same route as the American Elm. For many years it seemed that Slippery Elm was resistant to the blight and that only the American Elm would succumb. However, in the past ten years this has proven false, as more and more of the Slippery Elms are showing signs of the disease.

(This article was written over ten years ago and even in this short time, 20-25% of the existing population of Slippery Elm around my farm has died.)

Virtually all of the older American Elms in the area have died. There remain a few young trees, but they are decreasing in number rapidly. The Elms seem to get the disease at about fifteen years old, then die off in a two-year period, but I have seen younger trees affected with the disease as well. In the last several years, I have seen healthy trees turn brown and defoliate in midsummer, and die within a month. There seem to be other disease at work here now. I hope that people understand that this is an important species to plant to help ensure its survival.

Historical Background and Medicinal Uses

Slippery Elm is one of the most versatile plants in the herbal kingdom. An important tree of plenty, it is renowned for its beauty, medicine, and food; it seems to help everything it touches. Its herbal actions are demulcent, expectorant, emollient, diuretic, and nutritive in nature.

Slippery Elm has a long history of use as an herbal medicine; it is still listed as an official drug in the United States Pharmacopoeia and is also sanctioned as an over-the-counter drug. It is one of nature's best demulcents, its effectiveness proven through long use. It contains mucilage cells, starch, tannin, and calcium oxalate. These constituents penetrate and cover exposed and irritated surfaces, aiding in the healing process. Having emollient action, it tends to soften and relax inflamed tissues and is specified for inflamed conditions of mucus membranes of the bowels, stomach, throat, and kidneys. Its mucilage was employed by the Thomsonians during labor as a lubricant for midwives' hands. (Thompsonians are followers of a system of herbal medicine practiced by Doctor Samuel Thompson in the early 1900's.) Thomsonians also used Slippery Elm in combination with *Lobelia inflata* mixed with small amounts of soft soap to bring boils and abscesses to a head so they could be more easily lanced and drained. Slippery Elm also formed an important ingredient in an original Ojibwa treatment for cancer, now known as the Essiac formula, that is still widely used. It is reported that during the Revolutionary War, surgeons used the inner bark of Slippery Elm as a source for quick energy, and in 1776 soldiers who had lost their way in the frigid winter survived for twelve days on a jelly prepared with Slippery Elm and Sassafras. In times of starvation and hard winters, many native and pioneer peoples stayed alive by using the inner bark of this amazing tree as a food source.

Clearly, Slippery Elm is a tree of many uses. Its inner bark is excellent when prepared as a tea. In this form it can be used as an enema and as a vaginal douche for irritated membranes. The tea is also an effective wash for chapped hands and face. It's been used as a suppository by mixing the powdered bark with warm water and forming pieces about ½ inch thick by 1 inch long. The powder mixed with water makes an excellent poultice for wounds, burns, boils, and ulcers. The inner bark ground into a powder and prepared like a cereal with milk or water is recommended for an ulcerated stomach, general weakness, those recovering from illness, bleeding lungs, and bronchitis. Because of its mucilaginous nature, Slippery Elm's properties are readily available during the digestive process. Easily digested, it has as much nutrition as oatmeal, and is an excellent food source for infants and children with digestive disturbances. It is also a mild and painless laxative for children, with action so gentle it can be retained by the most sensitive stomach when no other food or medicine is tolerated. If desired, it may be flavored with cinnamon, nutmeg, or honey.

Slippery Elm is a superior medicine for sore throats and coughs. For the greatest effect, chewing on the soft inner bark while swallowing the mucilage is recommended. This is very helpful for a dry, non-productive cough.

Watching squirrels on spring walks, I learned to collect the young seeds and found them to be edible and delicious. Though this information is not available in any herbal guides I have read, I have experienced these tasty seeds to be perfectly palatable and safe. In recent herb classes, we sliced and braided the inner bark and made ropes, necklaces, and bracelets. They proved to be strong, but of course became slimy when wet. Perhaps a portable, self-worn combination skin care and respiratory tonic?

In conversation with David Winston, a well-known New Jersey herbalist, I confirmed my hunch that Slippery Elm was commonly used in non-medicinal ways by our First Nation People, who removed the mucilage and beat the fibers, then wove them into a rope, clothing, or covering.

Preparations and Dosage

There are many ways to prepare Slippery Elm bark; a few have already been mentioned. Some of the most common methods are listed here.

Tea
The general formula of two ounces of bark steeped in 1 quart of simmering water for 1 hour or longer. Strained and used freely, is good for both ingested teas and enemas.

Capsules
Finely powdered bark maybe encapsulated in gelatin or vegetable capsules. General recommendation is to take two capsules three times daily.

Poultice
To make a poultice, add warm water to the powder and make a thick, viscous paste. May be applied to wounds, burns, and boils to sooth and heal.

Nutritive Gruel
To make a nourishing gruel, bring one cup of milk to a simmer. Add 1 ½ teaspoons of powdered Slippery Elm and 1 teaspoon of honey to the milk and stir until it reaches the boiling point. Remove from the heat. Stir the gruel a few seconds more, adding a pinch of cinnamon powder if desired. This is delicious and very good for young children.

Elm Ooze
Whole pieces of bark may be simmered in a little water until a thick, gelatinous slime is produced. When cooled, this healing ooze may be used for raw, chapped skin and wounds.

Propogation and Cultivation

Given the current status of the Elm population in general, along with the incredible usefulness of Slippery Elm, it is imperative that we begin planting this tree as part of our sustainable farm and garden practices, much as we plant Comfrey and Jerusalem Artichokes. Though Slippery Elm is now very susceptible to Dutch Elm Disease, it seems to remain healthy for ten or fifteen years before contracting this disease. Thick young stands of trees can be thinned and used as medicine. Larger trees that have been infected by the disease will not recover and are good to harvest for medicine, building material, and firewood for a couple of years. Never harvest the inner bark from a healthy trunk, as this will allow access for disease. You may prune a few lower limbs to gather your medicine and not injure the tree.

Slippery Elm plantings should not only be considered for aesthetics and for food and medicine, but also as a source of seed stock to ensure the future survival of this most giving tree. Slippery Elm seeds may be sewn in their normal cycle in the spring of the year, in 18 inch raised peat moss, soil, and sand beds. The beds may need wire tops for protection of the young seeds and seedlings. You may expect some light germination that summer and a greater germination the following spring. Expect a 10-30% germination rate. Transplant the tree into tree tubes within the first month of germination (this soil should be a well-drained potting soil). They may be field planted after a year or two, depending on the size of your chosen tree tube. Always keep the tree watered during drought, and routinely check for insect predation and signs of fertilization needs.

At this juncture, I don't have enough information regarding how Slippery Elm is faring in other bio-regions. This information is necessary and will be useful in understanding the progression of Dutch Elm Disease. Slippery Elm is now susceptible to other diseases like Elm Phloem Necrosis, which is now in our bio-region. I am seeing healthy-looking Elm trees never recover and die by midsummer. Please pass any reports on to me at:

United Plant Savers Botanical Sanctuary
Attention: Paul Strauss
35703 Loop Road
Rutland, OH 45775

Harvesting

When possible, Slippery Elm should be harvested in the spring, when it is at its greatest potency. Make sure you have positively identified the correct species before harvesting. Many trees have a soft inner bark, but only Slippery Elm is so full of rich mucilage.

Always be conscious of the plant's energy, especially when harvesting material for medicine. Thanking the plant, or making an offering, keeps this process clear and open, thus recognizing the unseen reality that affects our existence so deeply. We as humans must recognize the value and energy of other life forms as much as our own. The proverb "do unto other as you would have others do unto you" should include the green world as well, and is most appropriate when harvesting medicine. These plants don't need us, we need them. Harvest only when there is an abundance of plant material. Never gather from roadsides, or polluted areas. Unless harvesting from an area being cleared for a road, building, or pond site, never girdle or strip the tree, as this will cause a sure death.

When gathering the inner bark of trees, harvest only from the branches, not the main trunk. In this way you will minimize damage to the tree. The preferred tool for gathering the inner bark is a draw knife, but a sharp pocket or kitchen knife will suffice for smaller amounts. To harvest, scrape away the outer bark, exposing the medicinal inner bark. Harvest it in 3-5 inch strips by angling the blade against the hard inner tissue and stoking downward. This is the same process used for gathering the inner bark of most medicinal trees, such as White Oak.

UpS Recommendations

Limit wild harvest to trees struck by natural disasters such as storms; otherwise use cultivated resources only. Possible substitutes include Marshmallow, Comfrey, and Mullien.

*This article originally appeared in *Planting the Future—Saving Our Medicinal Herbs,* edited by Rosemary Gladstar and Pamela Hirsch, and published by Healing Art Press, Rochester, VT. This is an important book for those interested in our disappearing medicinal herbs and how you can help sustain them.

Hackberry
Celtis occidentails
Elm Family
Sugar Berry or Nettle Tree

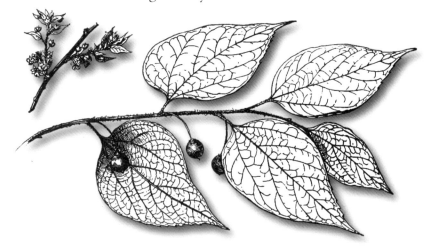

Hackberry is not very well known around here, but we are lucky to have some in our forests. It belongs to the Elm family, and is often mistaken for an Elm.

Adaptable to a variety of soil types, Hackberry does best in rich soils with a limestone underlayment where it can make fast growth. The younger trees have one of the most striking bark forms of any tree in our area—distinctively checkered, small, thick, corky plates. On older trees the bark smooths out and becomes thick with prominent ridges.

Hackberry fruit is purplish-brown and sweet when ripe. Birds love it, as do squirrels and raccoons. A great provider, Hackberry trees produce large numbers of berries; their predation is a major source for its seed dispersal.

As Hackberry's foliage begins to change, its green fruits ripen, turning orange to brown to blue-purple, and can stay on all winter long. The thin, pulpy covering is very sweet, hence its nickname, Sugarberry. I think it has a wonderful taste and in some years large quantities can be gathered. I have no doubt that our First Nation people used this as a food source. Dakota Tribes pounded the pulp and dried pits to season cooking meats.

The white kernel inside the seed's hard shell is sweet and soft, and also used as a food.

Hackberry leaves have a nettle-like look, thus one of its common names, Nettle tree. In autumn, the leaves turn a cheerful yellow. Interesting and common to this species is the "witch's broom," thick twiggy growths that come from a fungus mite cooperation that stimulates the distorted branching.

Its wood is heavy and light yellow, but soft and weak. Its lumber tends to twist. It has some use in the manufacture of boxes, crates, and inexpensive furniture.

Because of its adaptability, Hackberry is used in some city street plantings. This unique tree is easy to transplant and is a bonus to any yard, farm, or arboretum. It will attract wildlife and is wonderful to look at.

Hawthorn
Crataegus
The Rose Family

Our area has up to ten species of Hawthorn. They apparently cross easily, thus I have no single species listed. Hawthorn is a little tree with stiff, zig-zagging branches; it is well armed with long dangerous thorns, so when gathered together, Hawthorns can make impenetrable thickets. Be careful when working around Hawthorns—one of its thorns penetrating deep into the skin or a joint can lead to serious wound-pains for months. Hawthorn makes great nesting and cover sights for smaller birds due to its dense branching and thorns.

It has small white clusters of flowers that turn into half-inch diameter red or yellow fruits supported by slender stalks. The small fruit is eaten by both rodents and birds. Nimble-mouthed deer browse young twigs and leaves, as do domestic animals like sheep, goats, cattle, mules, donkeys, and horses. Herds will soon kill Hawthorn trees in pasture situations.

The Hawthorn fruit is well known in herbal medicine by our First Nation people and by Chinese and European herbalists who use it as a safe tonic for the heart. It has been used for angina, hypertension, arterial sclerosis, and reducing blood pressure. Its efficacy has been confirmed by controlled clinical studies.

Many beautiful varieties of Hawthorns are used for landscaping. The Washington Hawthorn is one of the best known. I have a nice one on this farm, doing well in an open location on the edge of a prairie.

Shagbark Hickory
Carya ovata
Juglandaceae
Walnut Family

Shagbark Hickory is a tall, straight-growing and long-lived tree—a vision of strength. A predominantly American tree, eleven of the twelve species of Hickory are found in the eastern half of the U.S. and only one species is found further west, with a range extending into Mexico. No other country has native Hickories. Along with Oaks, Hickories form one of the main climax forest members of our area. As Michael Snyder notes in a northernwoodlands.org article, "a climax forest is one that has escaped disturbance by forces like storms or diseases or logging long enough to have settled into a condition of relative stability."

The Shagbark and Shellbark Hickory have grey bark that is shed in tough vertical strips. This striking look makes it easy to identify in the forest. This shagging bark is one of the main homes for the endangered Indiana bat. Bitternut and Mockernut are smooth-bark Hickories also found on the Sanctuary.

Though hard to imagine, Hickories are slower growing than White Oak. Shagbark Hickories have large, alternate compound leaves comprising of five to seven leaflets, the end leaflet being the largest. These leaves are aromatic when crushed. In winter, Shagbark Hickory's large ½ inch leaf buds are another clue to its identity. If the summer is dry, its fall coloration is brown, but in a year of decent moisture the leaves turn a striking rich yellow.

Few trees rival the Hickory for both utility and food. Hickory wood is unequalled for handles and implements such as axes, sledge hammers, framing hammers, and madoxes, all of which must resist great strain and pounding. Like Oak and Ash, thin strips are woven into strong baskets. Its branches are used in the manufacturing of chairs and small tables. And for firewood, there's no wood better than seasoned Hickory. A cord of Hickory is equal to the energy of 1.12 tons of coal or 175 gal of oil. Hickory has always been recognized for its value in the smoking of meat. To try this, soak some of its shagging bark and place it on your fire right before putting the meat on.

A Hickory tree will only start producing nuts at about forty years old. Squirrels, turkeys, wood ducks, chipmunks, fox, deer, bear, and raccoon all devour its nuts. Deer will also feed on it leaves and young shoots. Squirrels are the main agents of the trees dispersal; they just can't remember where they buried all those nuts! Hickory nuts, especially those of the Shagbark and Kingnut, were one of the most important foods for First Nation people living within its range. They ate it "out of hand," made it into a drink, and pounded it into a mix-meal with cornmeal. Settlers learned the use of these nuts from First Nation people. In the fall it is easy to find the four-parted husks dropping away from the angled nuts.

Today Hickory boards are in fashion and are used in the manufacturing of kitchen cabinets. For all of its strength, Hickory decays quickly once it is downed. On the UpS Sanctuary we are fortunate to have many centenarian Hickories; some of our hills are predominated by these old beings. Dad's Woods, on the Medicine Trail, was named for being reserved by Lee Wood senior for his own hunting. Its abundance of game attracted to the

Hickory nuts made him a good provider. Certainly one of the reasons we have so much wildlife on the Sanctuary is because of its plenitude of older Hickories.

If you are lucky, in early fall you may find one of Americas largest caterpillars, the Hickory Horned Devil, a fearsome-looking 5-7 inch long, green and red-spined caterpillar that is the larva of the Regal or Royal Walnut Moth.

Hickory Horned Devil on Shagbark leaves

Shellbark Hickory or Kingnut Hickory
Carya laciniosa

Shellbark is similar to Shagbark Hickory, but prefers the deeply fertile, moist soils of our bottom lands. Shagbark does fine in drier soils. The Shellbark Hickory resembles the Shagbark, but generally has seven leaflets rather than five. Its edible nuts are the largest of all Hickory nuts, up to three inches long in the husks. Its wood is used like Shagbark Hickory.

Bitternut Hickory or Yellowbud Hickory
Carya cordiformis
Smoothbark Hickory

The Bitternut Hickory does well in rich bottomlands and in drier hillside soils. This a common tree in our forest. It is without the exfoliating bark of the Shagbark, and has seven to nine leaflets. Its wood is used similarly as Shagbark. As its name implies, its smaller, bitter-tasting nuts are not used by humans and are also less favored by animals. It is the most widely distributed of our Hickories.

Mockernut Hickory
Carya tomentosa
Smoothbark Hickory or Bigbud Hickory or White Hickory

This is mainly a tree of dry hillsides; it needs well-drained soils to thrive. Its leaf has a hairy stalk with five to seven leaflets. Its nuts are small-sized, with an extra thick and hard shell. The sweet kernels are difficult to get at, which is where the common name, Mockernut, came from. It has similar properties of wood as the Shagbark Hickory.

Pignut Hickory
Carya glabera
Smoothbark Hickory

Pignut is at home in dry ground and hillsides. It never attains the great girth of Shagbark. Its nut is thin-shelled and bitter, hence its name, Pignut. The leaves have to five to seven leaflets. Its wood possesses the same qualities as other Hickories.

Honeylocust
Gleditsia tricanthos
Legume Family
Sweetlocust

Honeylocust are tall trees known for their large, three-branched thorns along their trunk and main limbs. At one time, these thorns were used for carding wool. Occasionally a thornless tree occurs. Honeylocust is a good tree to have nearby, but well outside of your lawn or gardens because its thorns can be dangerous to the human body—yet it is always beautiful and always interesting.

Honeylocust is a lowland tree and prefers rich, well-drained soil. The alternate leaves are feathery and fern-like and tropical in character. They move in even the slightest of breezes, which is one of the tree's many outstanding features. The leaves come in late spring and turn a beautiful clear yellow before dropping in early fall. They are nearly full-grown when the fragrant blossoms appear. These tiny greenish, bell-shaped flowers are hard to see, but easily heard as they are mauled by bees and other nectar-loving insects. The seed pods are long and flattened. Honeylocust gets its name from the sweet, gummy pulp that is inside the pods when they are young. One must figure out how to get around those formidable thorns on its trunk for a taste. As fall approaches, this pulp gets bitter and dries around the shiny black seeds. The purple-brown, twelve to thirteen-inch long pods cling and rattle in the wind long after the yellow leaves have fallen. Time gives these pods S curves so when they fall the winds disperse them by whirling them along till they finally lodge and release their seeds. Cold, wet winters stratify these seeds so they may sprout.

Deer, rabbit, squirrel, and cattle will eat the Honeylocust fruit. Deer and cattle will also eat the seedlings and saplings. Honeylocust wood is hard, heavy, and durable in contact with soil, though not as durable as sound Black Locust *(Rabinia psudeocasia)*. It has been made into wheel hubs, fence posts, and firewood. With the demise of the Black Locust species on my farm, I have used Honeylocust boards for the steps to one of the outhouses, and to replace carpenter bee-damaged facia boards on the camp kitchen. If abundant, Honeylocust can serve effectively as an alternative for many of the uses of Black Locust.

There are thornless varieties planted throughout our cities in temperate climates. Honeylocust cannot exist in dense woods where there is not enough light. Below the Medicine Trail on Buckeye Lane, I watched four or five beautiful, mature Honeylocust trees die as the forest grew around and over them.

The ornamental characteristic of this tree, and the fact that it has few insect enemies and grows quickly in good locations, have made it muchplanted in public parks here and in Europe. Importantly, it does not get the Locust Borer that has so affected our Black Locust species.

American Hornbeam
Caprinus caroliniana
Corylaceae
Ironwood–Musclewood–Blue Beech

Never large but certainly sinuous, the fluted muscular ridges of its multiple trunks make Musclewood one of our most striking understory shrubs. Its blue-grey bark gives its common name, Blue Beech. Its other common name, Ironwood, is confusing since another member of its family, Hops Hornbeam, is also called Ironwood.

Shade tolerant, American Hornbeam is found growing in rich, moist locations and is commonly found along creek banks. The small, delicate birch-like leaves are strong, ribbed, pointed, and ovate. Wearing a many-shaded cloak of red and orange, it is a beautiful sight in autumn. The flowers grow in catkins, and its seed somewhat resemble a tiny-lobed Maple leaf with a small attached nutlet. This seed often hangs on into winter.

Though rarely straight-trunked, shorter pieces of Hornbeam trunk and branches make good tool handles and wedges, with wood even harder than Hickory. Although it decays quickly upon contact with soil, it does make good seasoned firewood. Its seeds are eaten by birds and squirrels, while deer browse its twigs and leaves. Its beauty makes American Hornbeam a wonderful landscaping species as it is most interesting to look at in all seasons.

Eastern Hops Hornbeam
Ostyra virginiana
Corylaceae
Ironwood – Leverwood

Growing a bit more upland, the Hop Hornbeam has similar needs as our other Hornbeam, *Caprinus caroliniana,* which is also found here. Slow growing, it is always a small slender tree that usually has a straight trunk with branching starting ⅓ the way up. Hop Hornbeam has a shaggy red brown bark formed of narrow shreds. This unique characteristic makes identification easy. The hops name derives from nutlets inside loose papery sacs that form a cone-like structure resembling hops. The word Hornbeam refers to the fact that its wood was traditionally used for making ox yokes.

Hop Hornbeam leaves are birch-like and turn a soft yellow in autumn. Its flowers are catkins that reach full growth in the first season and fruit in the second. These nutlets are less foraged upon than those of the American Hornbeam.

Since Hops Hornbeam is a small tree that does not occur abundantly, it is only used locally and is never found in the commercial market. Being harder than Oak, Hickory, or Locust, its wood is excellent for levers or handles that must endure great strain.

This is a little tree that any pioneer would be glad to have growing on his woodlot and is one of the most interesting understory trees in our local forests.

Cucumber Magnolia
Magnolia acumunata
Magnoliaceae
Cucumber Tree

Even though the Cucumber Tree is the hardiest and most wide-spread of our native Magnolias, it is not a common species here. There are no Cucumber Magnolias on the Goldenseal Sanctuary trails, and most people will never come in contact with this beautiful tree.

Where the Cucumber Magnolia grows is usually wonderful soil for woodland medicinal herbs. In Root Rock Holler, I am lucky to have many old Cucumber Trees living next to large old Tulip Poplars, Slippery Elm, Sugar and Red Maples. At their feet are vast amounts of Goldenseal, Ramps, and Black and Blue Cohosh.

A lover of rich well-drained soils, Cucumber Magnolia leaves get quite large, at six to ten inches. The flowers, with a yellowish-green color, can scarcely be seen among the new leaves. The name derives from the fleshy cones that resemble cucumbers—these fruits turn from greenish to pink then red as they mature. In September, the scarlet seeds hang out on threads waiting for the wind to release them. These spicy seeds are eaten by birds and rodents. Like other Magnolias, its leaves, buds, and inner bark have a wonderful sweet smell.

Another of our native trees, the Tulip Poplar is also a member of the Magnolia family and, like the Cucumber tree, it also releases a wonderful scent when its bark is broken or its leaves crushed.

Cucumber Magnolias have thin, furrowed, slightly scaly dark-brown bark. It is often cut alongside Tulip Poplar. Its lumber is sometimes used in cabinetmaking.

Because of its hardiness and ability to tolerate different climactic conditions, the Cucumber Tree is often grown in parks and arboretums as an ornamental. It can be used as root stock to graft less hardy Magnolias. It is easily grown and tolerates transplanting. It also has the ability to stump-sprout back after being cut or damaged.

Its soft, weak wood is light colored and was used at one time in the making of boxes and crates. I have run into references to the whole Cucumber-like seed pod being placed in brandy, vodka, or moonshine in Appalachian farmsteads and used as a tonic tincture for what ails ya.

Red Maple
Acer rubrum
Aceraceae
Scarlet Maple

Red Maple is one of the most common tree species in eastern North America. Around the farm in the early spring, Red Maple is our earliest plant to produce flowers in great numbers, with Silver Maple and Elm at its heels. It flowers long before its leaves appear. This is important for our early insect foragers, especially honeybees, which need a lot of early pollen and nectar to build hive populations to assist in harvesting the summer flow.

Along with Silver Maple, Red Maple is classified as a soft Maple. It is not as strong and does not live as long as Sugar Maple. Red Maple displays some red in all seasons. Spring's first flower burst is red, the early leaves are red, its seed wings are red, and in fall, it has a showy display of brilliant crimson leaves. When leaves fall, it shows red buds and twigs. It was Henry David Thoreau's favorite tree.

Red Maple can thrive in wet or dry upland sites, and the beaver that moved into one of my reclamation pond sites loved it. It does stump-sprout profusely when cut. Young trees have smooth gray bark, and are confused by some with Beech at this stage. On older trees the bark is rough and scaly, separating into shaggy plates. There are two notable Red

114

Maples on the property that were never cut; these centenarians look nothing like the younger trees.

Nowhere in the entire world is there found in nature such magnificent foliage coloration as in our American deciduous forests. Red Maple is one of its main stars, among the riot of colors visible from space.

Most of our "curly maple" lumber comes from this species. It is the most widespread of all of our Maples.

In city plantings, Red Maple is particularly suited for use in narrow streets. Maple syrup can be made from its sap, but it has much less sugar than Sugar Maple. It is a far shorter-lived tree than Sugar Maple, and much faster-growing. Deer and rabbit eat the young leaves and shoots.

Silver Maple
Acer saccharium
Aceraceae
Water Maple or Soft Maple

This is a common lowland native species that usually grows in flood plains and wet soil. It is a fast-growing tree that rarely lives over one hundred years. Its weak, brittle wood breaks easily in storms. They have been extensively planted on city streets and farms for quick shade, but need constant pruning to make them safe.

The Silver Maple leaf is deeply dissected with a sliver-white underside, hence its common name. It flowers early and profusely before it leafs out. A boon to insects, the Silvers in my yard mean a loud buzz of bees for weeks in springtime. It has the largest winged seed of any native maple. One of its finest points is the graceful upturning of its branches. Fall coloration is a weak pale yellow—nothing as spectacular as Red and Sugar Maple. To its credit, it has long, somewhat flattened leaf stalks, so any movement of air sets its foliage dancing and spinning green to silver as its branches move up and down.

My farmhouse is 140 years old, and the main yard-tree planted back in the day for shade was the quick growing Silver Maple. I now refer to this tree as Big Maple, and I'm dealing with its slow death. It was three foot in diameter when I bought the farm 42 years ago. It is now huge—six plus feet in diameter. I have had to prune every second year for the past ten years. As it breaks in storms, branches damage the summer kitchen and

116

main farmhouse slate roofs, which are integral to my catchment water system. The main trunk divides itself into two huge, two and a half foot diameter secondary trunks. The one angling towards the house is now dead and gone. I had to cable this side long ago because if it went, it would take out half my house. During big storms, I never slept in my downstairs bedroom.

To its credit, limbs hollowed out by heart rot create excellent housing for birds, squirrels, and snakes (I love snakes, so this is no problem). Rodents, squirrels, and birds feed on its seeds. Deer browse its twigs and foliage.

Having lived so close to this tree, I will tell you some of my experiences with it. Many years ago, before it got so huge, I would let its upturned branches come into my yard almost at eye level. One summer, a Ruby Throated Hummingbird made her tiny cup of a nest on the tips of the lowest branches. She got used to me and the dogs, and I would always lovingly acknowledge her in passing. Maybe she was young and new to this nesting thing to dare to be so close, out on a limb so to speak.

Snakes, Hummingbirds, Bees

In spring, we get powerful thunderstorms. I can remember my amazement watching the hummingbird from my living room window as her nesting branch was blown crazily by a particularly heavy storm. It was hard to make her out in her nest; she was but a fast-moving blur in the extreme tossing and bouncing, and the horizontal rain that was upon the farm pummeled her. I remember that I caught 2,000 gallons of water in that hour-long storm. Yet afterwards, she was fine, still in her nest upon her eggs. Taking that pounding was just part of her job. It happened again just after her eggs hatched, and she rode out that storm as well—this time protecting her kids, who were taking the ride of their lives under the tiny noble breast of their mom. No big deal.

I was leaning on Big Maple talking to my mom's ninety-year-old boyfriend, Sam, as he swung on the hammock, when right between us, two black snakes entwined in copulation dropped from a branch ten feet above our heads. The fall, and the loud thump they made, did not slow them down at all. Prime directive was in full control. Fully entwined and moving like a barber shop pole, they finished their coupling before splitting apart and moving off in their own directions.

For many years, on the furthest reaches of the highest branches of Big Maple, Baltimore Orioles would make their hanging-sack nests. In winter or the following spring a nest would fall and I would examine it. Most of it was woven together from my horse's hair that they had harvested from the fence lines.

It was a hot summer day and the Orioles had been feeding their clutch for a week. I was stepping off the porch when I noticed a six-foot black snake at the base of Big Maple—half its body erect, and flashing its tongue (I have seen much bigger black snakes on the farm). I decided to sit and watch. The tree was 75 feet tall then, forked at ten feet and then forked many, many times to its top. I watched that black snake climb up Big Maple, and take the correct fork every time, without stopping, to reach the nest 70 feet high. The snake's weight bent the thin, small top branch, so the snake was inverted head down, tail wrapped around the branch. The hopeless parents tried to drive the snake off to no avail. It was a difficult but amazing sight as the black snake cleaned out the nest. Quite phenomenal that the snake knew exactly where to go and made all of the correct moves, never stopping once from where he first ascended the tree from the ground; some powerful senses at work here.

Before I even knew the words Tracheal Mite, I always had ten to twenty beehives in my backyard. Our very first profusely-flowering plant near the hives was always Big Maple. I saw it bloom on warm days at the end of February once, but that is too early and there were not many seeds that year. In bloom, it becomes a buzzing tree of honey bees gathering the goods to build hive strength. Pollen is the protein, and honey is the energy to feed the larva.

In May, a hive's strength can be so great (up to 50,000 bees) that the bees divide and swarm with a new queen. Swarming is a natural instinct that helps ensure the survival of the species. After flying around the yard crazily, they all light (land) when the queen picks a good spot. From here they send out scouts to find their new home. The queen would often choose to land about 20 feet off the ground on the end of a small limb on Big Maple. A swarm in May is a valuable catch—three pounds or more hanging in a good swarm up to 2 feet long. They have a ton of energy to build their hive quickly, and a local saying goes, "a swarm in May is worth a barn full of hay."

To hive these swarms was a fun spring adventure. I first set up a ladder that would give me access to the swarm's limb. I would tie a 50 foot piece of rope about four feet away from the swarm on its branch, and then put the rope over the branch just above it. I step on the rope and use two hands to cut the swarm's limb six inches beyond the tie, throw the pruner to the ground, and slowly lower the swarm limb within six inches of a brood box waiting on the ground. In the brood box, I put some honey drizzling and rub the inside fo the box with lemon balm leaf (*Melissa oficinalis,* Melissa is Latin for bee). I tie off the rope, climb down the ladder, and with one vigorous shake, drop the bees into their new home. I did this several times and it never failed. No gloves, no veil. When bees swarm they are not aggressive, which makes this job easier. They now make long poles with bags for swarm catchers. I like my method because of the process I went through to figure it out, necessity being the mother of invention and self-satisfaction.

It is 2011 as I write this, and once again in the late fall I have had to take out more of Big Maple's rotted limbs. With the tree so much smaller, it won't have to expend as much energy sending nutrients skyward. It can't have many years left. I planted some replacement shade trees years ago, but it will be a long time before they do the work as well as Big Maple, a tree whose life provided so much life. My perfect neighbor.

Sugar Maple
Acer saccharine
Aceraceae
Hard Maple or Rock Maple

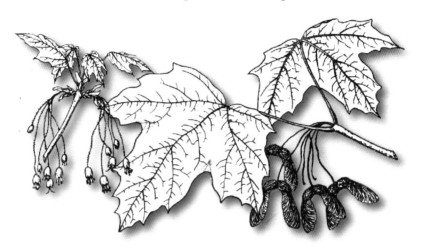

Tall and handsome, the Sugar Maple is one of America's best known, most beautiful and beloved species. Even though its range is the Northeastern two-thirds of the U.S., it is often thought of as a New England tree. The attributes most people know are its brilliant red, yellow, and gold fall colorations and the sweet goodness of maple syrup. It can grow in a variety of soil types, but does best in deep, well-drained loam.

Like the rest of the Maple family, this is a handsome tree in all seasons. Stately, its dark-gray bark has ridges and thick-curled plates. Sugar Maple blooms after our Red and Silver Maples and produces flowers in great abundance. As the leaves unfurl, the greenish-yellow flowers hang gracefully on long, thread-like stems. Striking in the spring, the tree can be hidden in a haze of its own profuse flowering.

The Sugar Maple is long-lived and tolerant of shade, its seedlings patiently waiting for their time to reach the sun-exposed canopy. Its calcium-rich leaf litter helps to create the limey soil the tree needs. I am always thankful for those who bag up Maple leaves in local towns and cemeteries in the fall for disposal. I gladly gather their bags because Sugar Maple is the best leaf I know to use as a garden mulch and cover.

The main uses of its whitish lumber has always been for furniture and flooring. Drying harder than Oak, it was used extensively for roller skating rinks, bowling alleys, gymnasium floors, and cutting boards.

I have had to harvest larger Sugar Maples that were ripped in two by wind and ice storms on the farm's ridge tops. I was able to harvest the main log for milling; the top branches, too small to mill, make hot-burning firewood.

Although slow-growing, Sugar Maple makes a wonderful landscaping and street tree. We also have Black Sugar Maples in our forest, but they are so similar to Sugar Maples that they are easily confused. You will also notice herbs like Blue Cohosh and Ramps thriving in the Sugar Maple's dense shade and rich soil.

Maple syrup is now a multi-million dollar business. Originally, the art of tapping Maples was taught to settlers by First Nation people. It is a slow process, and one must boil forty gallons of sap down to make one gallon of syrup. In late winter or early spring, a broken branch will have an icicle this can be sucked on like a frozen popsicle—not very sweet, but still with the hint of maple syrup. The sap itself has been used as a spring tonic, and maple syrup can be used in the making of cough syrups. First Nation people would use the inner bark as a tea to treat diarrhea and coughs, and to help kidney flow.

Maple syrup is full of minerals. A wonderful, natural electrolyte replacement can be made using 16 oz. of spring or carbonated spring water, or coconut water. Add the juice of one good-sized lemon, 2 tablespoons of maple syrup, and a touch of cayenne for the adventurous. I drink it cold when working on hot summer days. This drink is perfect to have on hand when you are putting up hay in scorching temperatures.

In Root Rock Holler, there are many stately, mature Sugar Maples three to four feet in diameter. They soar a hundred feet up and out of the Holler, with branching starting halfway up the trunk. So far, most of these have withstood high winds and ice damage.

Black Oak
Quercus veluntina
Fagaceae

Black Oak, along with Red Oak *(Quercus rubra),* are common trees in the east and mid-west and share many identifying characteristics. All have points on their leaf tips and produce mature acorns every two years. Although Black and Red Oak both need well-drained soil, they are somewhat separated within the forest, with Red Oak favoring richer soils and Black Oak better able to handle poorer soil. Black Oak acorns are small, bitter, and not foraged upon like those of the White Oak grouping. Black Oak has a darker and tighter bark with no flattening patterns like Red Oak. In our area, its bark gets more lichen growth than the Red and is not as graceful and symmetrical in its growth; it has the habit of shedding its lower limbs throughout its life. Black and Red Oaks can cross, forming a hybrid.

The inner bark of the Black Oak is yellow or orange. This substance is quercitron and in the days before aniline dyes this was America's main yellow dye. A common sight for many years was the hulks of large Black Oaks left rotting on the forest floor after only their inner bark was harvested.

Apparently Black Oak was the favorite fuel for early American potters, as it certainly supplies more BTUs than Red Oak, burns very hot, and leaves little ash.

Black Oak's late fall coloration is yellow. If there has been any autumn rain the Black Oak woods next to Heart Pond can be quite lovely, even into November.

Though not as versatile as White Oak or as beautiful as Red Oak, I have used Black Oak lumber for several building projects and it is holding up well. The Sulfur Shelf mushroom, also known as Chicken of the Woods, are often found on Black Oaks. Thirty-plus pound wheelbarrow loads are not uncommon. Although my friends and I cook and eat Sulfur Shelf mushrooms regularly with no problems, some people report digestive disturbances when eating this mushroom species.

Chestnut Oak
Quercus prinus
Fagaceae
Rock Oak

A slow-growing lover of our rocky hillsides and ridge tops, Chestnut Oak leaves resemble those of the American Chestnut tree. The "Rock Oak" is a member of the White Oak grouping whose properties it shares. Its lumber is exceptionally tough and strong, and durable enough for outdoor applications; color-wise, its lumber has more brown in it than *Quercus alba*. Unlike the other White Oaks, its handsome bark is dark and deeply furrowed. At one time its bark was widely used for tanning.

Branching starts far up the trunk, which can attain great heights. Overall, the tree is a vision of Herculean strength. Chestnut Oak leaves are firm and thick. The underside of the leaf is more pale in color than the top and the whole leaf turns yellow in the fall. Its acorns are egg-shaped, much larger than White Oak and heavily foraged upon by deer, squirrels, turkey, chipmunk, and grouse.

Chestnut Oak is one of the most common and beautiful oaks in our area. It must be admired for its ability to tolerate and thrive in tough growing conditions.

During an especially heavy wind storm, a two-trunked Chestnut Oak was toppled; each trunk was 3 feet in diameter and eighty feet long. For a hundred years it had watched over the valley above the Cave of the Fallen Cow. I would never cut such a beautiful tree, it was a gift of nature, a tree I knew intimately for forty years. With the help of my neighbor, Paul Neidhart—our forest trails conveniently join—we hauled the trunks to his diesel sawmill and made 2-inch thick plank flooring for my daughter Alana's solar cabin. The tops were kept to be used as Shitake mushroom logs, and other parts for firewood—giving it a chance to release its accumulated solar energy (as all energy is solar, after all).

Life goes on in the hundreds of acres of woodlands that own me. It seems that there is always more than enough wood that has fallen or died naturally for all my building and heating needs. We use it for campfires for visiting students, events, gatherings, sweat lodge, and hot tub fires.

Chinkapin Oak
Quercus muehlenbergii
Fagaceae
Yellow Oak

Chinkapin Oak is another member of the White Oak grouping. Its bark is grayer and flakier than *Quercus alba,* and in this area, Chinkapin Oak is much less populous. Its sweet acorns are small but can be eaten out of hand often without leeching their tannins. Its leaves also resemble a Chestnut leaf. Chinkapin Oak's wood qualities are similar to *Quercus alba.* It grows best on limestone seams in our forest.

Post Oak
Quercus stellate
Fagaceae

Another member of the White Oak grouping is the Post Oak—again not as plentiful as *Quercus alba*. Its leaves are noticeable because of their Maltese Cross shape. Like our Virginia Pine, it is happy to grow upon poor, dry, over-pastured hillsides with little topsoil. Its common name is a testimony to its legendary strength. Post Oak is always much smaller and scrubbier looking than *Quercus alba,* its branches twisted and gnarled. It loses many branches as it ages, leaving impressive scars on its trunk. When rebuilding the hundred-plus-year-old stock and hay barn on the farm in 1982, I used Post Oak for the new king posts.

Swamp White Oak
Quercus bicolor
Fagaceae

This is another member of the White Oak family that occurs naturally in our area and we have used for landscaping. As its name implies, it is doing well next to our creeks and ponds. White on the under-side of its leaf (hence the Latin name bicolor) it is faster-growing than *Quercus alba*.

White Oak
Quercus alba
Fagaceae
Beech Family

In six thousand years of recorded history, humans have had a total of 43 years of world peace, which is pitiful. I find the human species interesting but deeply faulted and invasive; basically we just can't get along easily. Of all the species on this planet the stately White Oak, along with the Humpback Whale, are my favorites. I would miss them terribly if they disappeared. As a child, the White Oak was the first plant whose strength and presence I could feel and know beyond just its name.

White Oak is not the tallest of our hardwoods—Poplar takes that claim. A Sycamore can obtain a larger girth. But there is no other tree I know of that shows the kind of strength and nobility endowed within our White Oak. A very slow-growing tree, White Oak offers so much to so many in so many different ways. It can have huge horizontal branching up to fifty feet long. Unlike the Black Oak family, White Oaks produce acorns every year, and their leaf tips are rounded, whereas the Black/Red Oak group have pointed tips. White Oak acorns have been a staple food for many First Nation people for eons, and are a wildlife magnet favored by deer, bear, squirrel, and turkey. Squirrels bury acorns near the trees they are foraging and never remember all of their treasures, making them great propagators. Blue Jays have developed along with the White Oak species—they have a physical adaptation in their mouths that allows them to carry multiple acorns far from the foraged tree. Jays have been responsible for greatly expanding White Oak's range over time.

Quercus alba offers beauty in every season. Young leaves first appear in the spring as bright red, then turn pink, and then silvery white. In autumn, the leaves turn scarlet and can hang on into winter. In early spring and late winter, when bared of its leafy cloak, it is impossible not to feel the White Oak's presence with its striking white bark and horizontal branching. It is a picture of forest nobility.

White Oak is the most utilitarian of all our hardwoods. It is a primary choice in almost every possible use for wood. It can be easily split into hot-burning firewood, is used in tanning, and is the best wood for tight cooperage, such as barrels to hold liquids like wine, whisky and brandy. When in contact with the soil, it is long lasting and is used for barn posts and fence posts. And, of course, it is highly prized for flooring, shingles, and furniture.

White Oak was the favored wood in the days of wooden sailing ships; over sixty acres of century-old White Oak were needed to build one ocean-going vessel. The legendary strength of the Revolutionary War ships like "Old Ironsides"—the *U.S.S. Constitution*—was dependant upon White Oak. My hundred-plus year old barns have White Oak siding and hand-hued oak beams. On the solar cabin the Oak deck, which is exposed to all weather, has been down for almost thirty years with only a little mainte-nance. White Oak is also a great wood for most farm tools and imple-ments. I could go on and on, but you get the point. This is one useful, gorgeous tree!

The inner bark of White Oak is one of the world's great astringent medi-cines. It is used for diarrhea, seeping sores, hemorrhoids, internal hemor-rhaging, gum disorders, and poison ivy. The tree's medicine should always be harvested from branches, not the trunk.

White Oak is a perfect wood for Shitake mushroom production. This past fall we harvested twenty pounds of Hen of the Woods mushrooms from a large dead White Oak. Hen of the Woods is both a delicious food and a valuable medicine which seems to prefer White Oak stumps. I often find these the size of basketballs. They taste better than the Sulpher Shelf (Chicken of the Woods) and I use them as an ingredient in my Ginseng Ginger and Three-Fungi Extract.

In the Appalachians, both high and low-grade White Oak is being harvested at an alarming rate for such a slow-growing tree. Much of the high grade is not even milled in this country, but is sent overseas where it is cached in deep cold water and stored for later use. Much of the low-grade wood goes for chips for pulp, and for pallet production, where it is used once and then sent to landfills. As younger and younger trees are cut, the gene pool of this amazing tree is being diminished. We humans are tragically short-sighted in this. Our world will be a poorer place without this noble species. In the past ten years I have seen more and more White Oaks that seem healthy just die in a short time. I worry—could this be the arrival of Sudden Oak Death disease (Ramorun Blight)?

I dearly love this tree and would often go up to a young White Oak grove that I have watched growing since moving to this farm 42 years ago. Back then, this grove's Mother Oak was still alive, six foot in diameter, listing at a 45-degree angle over a creek. This Monarch served as my evening perch after work. Protected in her 35-foot arms, all was perfect, my life on the right track. My hope for you is that you may find your Oak.

*A must read for all tree lovers is the book by William Logan, *Oak, The Frame of Civilization*

Red Oak
Quercus rubra
Fagaceae

R ed Oak is a large tree and is one of our more common Oaks. A member of the Black Oak group, it thrives in rich, well-drained soil. This group produces mature acorns every two years, and their leaves have bristly pointed tips, unlike the rounded tips of White Oak leaves. Red Oak bark is separated into shiny flat-topped ridges. In the furrows just under the bark is a reddish layer, another of its unique characteristics. The acorn has a saucer shaped cup; the nut is oblong, about an inch long. Unlike plentiful and tasty White Oak acorns, Red Oak's white kernel is bitter and is rarely foraged upon. Deer will browse the young buds and twigs in the winter as a food source.

The Red is one of our fastest-growing Oaks, and one of the longest lived. A beautiful tree beloved for its wine-colored autumn leaves, it is planted not just in U.S. parks, but is also a great favorite overseas. Red Oak has the ability to sprout vigorously when cut or burned, thereby aiding reforestation.

Red Oak leaves are extremely variable in shape, even on the same tree. Members of the Red and Black Oak group hybridize easily, making identification difficult.

Though a beautiful red-tinged lumber, Red Oak does not have the characteristics of White Oak's toughness, strength, or its resiliency in contact with soil and weather. It is a much lighter and porous wood than White Oak. It is commonly used in flooring, furniture, and slack cooperage (barrels for hard items, but not water), and for many general building purposes. It is a much easier wood to work (e.g., cut, plane, and sand) than White Oak. Its beauty and rapid growth make this tree important and rewarding to plant.

I am lucky to have another variety of Red Oak growing on my property, the striking Scarlet Oak *(Quercus coccinea)*. It has thinner, more sharply-pointed and deeply-lobed leaves than the Red Oak, and deeper magenta fall coloration. Its leaves can last late into winter. It has smaller branches than *Quercus rubra* and forms a narrow, irregular crown.

The unusual-looking species Squaw Root, also known as Cancer Root *(Conopholis americana)* parasitizes Red Oak in our woods. Cancer Root, as a member of the Broom Rape family, lacks chlorophyll and has scale-like leaves. Cancer Root was collected by First Nation people as a food source, but I have bitten into the raw *Conopholis* and can't imagine anybody using this plant raw. It must need cooking to make it palatable. As far as I can see, it was regarded as a cancer on Oak roots.

Cancer Root

131

Haircut

In 1972 my friend and physical plane teacher Bill Clonch asked me to help load a huge five-foot diameter, eight-foot long Red Oak log onto our one-ton Chevy truck to take to the mill. We had no large equipment to do a dangerous job like this, but counted on gravity to get it done. The truck was parked just below a bank upon which the log sat. From the log to the truck, we set four 3x10x12 White Oak planks at a shallow grade to move the log to the truck. With large canthooks we started the log down the ramps, stopping it with wedge-shaped blocks if it started moving too fast. I was twenty-two with long hair tied in a ponytail hanging a third of the way down my back. Slowly and successfully we had moved the immense log half the way to the truck bed. As I was working on this hot summer day my ponytail came undone, cutting my peripheral vision. Bill noticed that one of our wedge blocks had split as the log ran over it with its massive weight. He shouted a sharp warning to jump back, which I did just as the log missed me by inches, nearly turning me into Pancake Paul. Bill's correct, loud, and immediate response was, "Goddamn it boy, you nearly died because of that damn long hair!" The day's work was over as the runaway log had taken out the truck's sideboards and fallen to the ground; luckily, it was stopped by a 16-inch single mulboard plow before it could take out the side of Bill's barn. I set down my canthook, realizing what a close call it had been. I went into Bill's house and had Retha cut my damn hair off. That was the last day I had long hair, and have never missed it since.

Osage Orange
Maclura pomifera
Mulberry Family
Hedgeapple-Bowwood

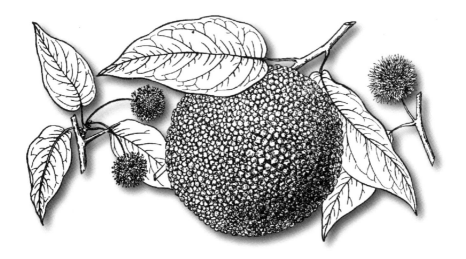

Osage Orange is a monotypic genus, containing only the single species. It is native to North America, with its original home in the bottomlands of the Arkansas and Red River valleys. Now it is naturalized across much of the south, the Appalachians, and north to Pennsylvania and New York.

Osage is a medium-sized tree with bark the color of burnt orange. The trunk is usually short, dividing into limbs with curved branches. When cut, it displays a deep orange heartwood, and with its curvy nature it can be hard to find a straight piece. This tree is armed with stout spines, which make it difficult to handle. Like Hawthorn, the thorns can cause infection if embedded deeply into skin or a joint. Be careful when handling this tree.

Osage roots are covered by an orange-colored bark. Its leaves are alternate, very shiny, 3-5 inches long, and 2-3 inches wide. They are thick and firm and turn a beautiful, clear bright yellow in late autumn.

Hedgeapple, as it is regionally known, seems to have no insect enemies. A broken leaf has a characteristic milky juice, while the large, softball-sized fruits also contain a milky juice. The fruits carry a citrus/cedar smell and are covered by small rounded protrusions resembling very rough oranges. Growing up in New York, we called the fruits Monkey Brains, and would of course throw them at each other.

The migration of Osage Orange in human hands came by way of its extreme usefulness. It is named for the Osage Tribe of Arkansas and Missouri who made use of its incredibly heavy, strong, tough, yet flexible wood for their bows. So esteemed were they that single bows were traded equally for a horse, bridle, and blanket. War clubs were also made of its wood, as were the billyclubs used through the years by police departments.

It is a very hot-burning firewood, but be careful, it can pop and spark when air is introduced into the firebox of your woodstove. For the best railroad ties, nothing ever came close to Osage. Unfortunately, there are just not enough of them anymore.

Before the introduction of wire fencing, Hedgeapple created an impenetrable fence row due to its hardiness in heat, drought, and wind. These fences were "horse high, bull strong and pig tight" as a bit of local wisdom holds. Fence posts of Osage can last fifty-plus years—there are still remnant Osage hedge rows in my old fields and surrounding farms. These fences have mostly died because of the overtopping of the advancing forest that robs their sunlight. There were thousands of miles of Hedgeapple fence rows across America at one time.

Osage wood was made into hubs for the wheels of farm wagons. Woodworkers use it for dowel turning and its root bark was used to make a yellow dye. Bill taught me to use its wood for all of the single and double trees for our mules because of its incredible strength.

Osage Oranges seem to have the ability to keep cockroaches at bay—their strong aroma and milky latex may have something to do with this.

Not many animals eat its fruit, but some squirrels tear it apart to eat its seeds. Deer may browse it, but not often. It seems the tree reproduces more by its clonal sprouts than by its seed.

I call this valuable tree vegetable steel. When I find straight pieces, I use it for my fence posts. Some of these are now forty-plus years old and showing no rot. I used its lumber for the joists of my cabin deck, which are constantly out in all weather. I have many stand-alone trees and some small patches of Osage on this farm, so I can harvest small amounts as needed.

It is a slow grower and is not planted often anymore, so not much is ever available. The toxic treatment of wood for outdoor use could cease if enough supply of Osage Orange could be had.

It could be that in your area, Black Locust is not in demise as it is around here (see: *Another Appalachian Species*). Locust is faster growing, but also incredibly long-term durable in contact with the ground. I have sound Black Locust posts still on a fence line I built 35 years ago.

Stronger than Oak, tough as Hickory, and flexible as Ash, Osage Orange is a valuable wood indeed. Plant it and you will be glad you did. Osage remains sound even when dead—I'll be harvesting some this summer that has died because of being overtopped. It would have been smart, in the first five years on the farm, to have planted a ½ acre, but I was too busy for my own good. I would suggest to any young farmer that when you plant your first orchard, also plant this remarkable resource.

Pawpaw
Asimina triloba
Custard Apple Family

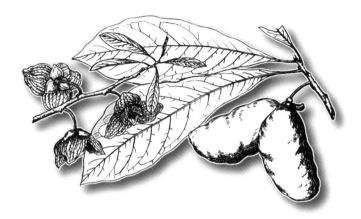

We are lucky to be in one of the areas of the United States to have such a large population of Pawpaws, which happens to be North America's largest native fruit tree. Pawpaw is a tropical fruit in a temperate climate, and is the most northern representative of the Custard Apple Family, related to 2,100 tropical fruits. One of its local nicknames is, in fact, Custard Apple.

The Pawpaw is an attractive small tree; the largest I have seen around here is twenty feet tall and a foot in diameter. In the south, I hear it can grow much larger. It is rare to find isolated trees; it especially likes the company of its own kind, and usually forms patches. The Pawpaw's wood is light and soft, greenish in color with streaks of brown and red. Its gray bark is thin and smooth; its tough fibrous inner bark was used by First Nation people and settlers for making mats, fish nets, and ropes.

All parts of this big herb, when bruised, have an acrid diesel-like smell disagreeable to most people, but I like its uniqueness. Its smell makes it very easy for students learning to identify trees and shrubs. Once you know a plant's smell you will never forget it—think of Sassafras, Yarrow, Spicebush, Plum Blossoms, Walnut leaves, and Lily of the Valley. I could go on, but Pawpaw is in this category.

Pawpaw leaves are large, tropical-looking, and oblong, 12-15 inches long, and 4-5 inches wide. The leaves are alternate on the branches and cluster in whirls on branch ends. An interesting fact—the small, flat, emerging leaves on the branch tips, known colloquially as "the Cinnamon Paintbrush bud," is what John Audabon used as his brush for his first paintings. When you feel this bud you can understand how perfect they are for fine detail. The leaf stalks are short and thick. Pawpaw leaves have always reminded me of a big ol' dog's wagging tongue.

Pawpaw flowers are down-turned and appear early in spring before the leaves. Because they can flower so early, a late frost will make for only small amounts of fruit. These ill-smelling flowers are solitary and bell shaped, with the fleshy drooping petals turned backward. They start green, turning an eye-catching deep maroon about 1½-2 inches in diameter. It is truly one of the most interesting and beautiful of our spring wild flowers. They are mostly pollinated by flies; a trick to produce more fruit is to put manure near the flowering trees.

The fruit is aromatic, hanging singly or in clusters in September. It is green and firm, turning yellow with black markings at maturity. It is soft and fleshy, and custard-like to eat. These sweet fruits are actively sought out by raccoon, opossum, squirrel, turkey, and bear.

The tree migrates by the seed being deposited in animals' manure. In the forest they rarely fruit, only the trees in the open and at the woods' edges make fruit. Some folks like me are satisfied to eat a few of them early when they start falling; some eat all they can find. Early settlers used the ripe fruit pulp to make a yellow dye.

Because in a good year the fruit is so prolific, and eaten by so many four-leggeds, we have large populations of Pawpaw in our understory. The flat brown seeds are about ¾-1 inch, highly polished, and have a wonderful feel to handle when dry in a bowl. They have insecticidal properties, and have been used as a rinse or shampoo for lice.

Some herb companies sell Pawpaw capsules for use in cancer therapy. I have heard of local folks using Pawpaw twig tea against cancer. I am not aware of any results. I read in *Medicinal Plants and Herbs* by Foster and Duke, that "Seeds [are] toxic and probably the leaves and bark contain potentially useful (anticancer), yet potentially toxic acetogenins." Before using this plant internally, do your research. These chemicals make Pawpaw naturally resistant to most insects, yet Pawpaws are the sole host of North America's longest-tailed swallowtail, the Zebra Swallow-tailed Butterfly. We have plenty of them around here.

Integrations Acres LTD, (www.integration acres.com), a business run and owned by Chris Chmiel, produces products from Pawpaws that are gathered, cultivated, and processed in Southern Ohio. It is the world's largest Pawpaw processor.

Chris has given me other interesting information about this remarkable plant. Pawpaw fruit is a super nutritious fruit. It has been tested and found to be higher than bananas, apples, and oranges in niacin, calcium, phosphorus, manganese, magnesium, iron, copper, zinc, protein, fat, and seven of the eleven essential amino acids. There are more antioxidants in half a Pawpaw then there are in a whole apple or pear. Because of its fragility and short shelf life, Pawpaws lend themselves to being processed and frozen for later use. Simply remove the skins and seeds, and then freeze. Frozen Pawpaw pulp can be turned into products like jam, popsicles, smoothies, ice cream, beer, and many other culinary creations.

In 1502, Spanish explorer Hernandez DeSoto made notations that in the Missouri River Valley, native peoples were propagating, harvesting, and processing the Pawpaw. If this fascinating tree has piqued your interest, then check out the Ohio Pawpaw Festival organized by Chris, which is held in Albany, Ohio every September during peak Pawpaw season. See *www.ohiopawpawfest.com*

This remarkable tree is a treasure trove in our ecosystem; it is beautiful, interesting, and historical; providing so much to so many who live near it. Today, there is a Pawpaw Foundation dedicated to promoting knowledge of the Pawpaw. Kentucky State University in Frankfort is the home of the USDA Pawpaw Germplasm Repository and Research.

And there is of course, the old American folk song even I knew as a child, "Way down yonder in the Pawpaw Patch:"

Where oh where is pretty little Susie?
Where oh where is pretty little Susie?
Where oh where is pretty little Susie?

Way down yonder in the Pawpaw patch

Picking up Pawpaws, putting 'em in her basket
Picking up Pawpaws, putting 'em in her basket
Picking up Pawpaws, putting 'em in her basket

Way down yonder in the Pawpaw patch

Come on boys, let's go find her
Come on boys, let's go find her
Come on boys, let's go find her

Way down yonder in the Pawpaw patch.

See you there in September.

Persimmon
Diospyros virginana
Ebonacea Family
Possum Wood

Persimmon is one of our most productive native food trees. This past fall (2007) on the trees just around my farm house were thousands of pounds of crazy-sweet fruit. Other than myself, the deer, opossums, and coons also feasted on them. That fall you could camp for a month by the flat at the bend in the creek and hunt, tan hides, and make a tribe's supply of Persimmon-fruit leather. You'd mix it with summer's rich harvest of berries, Hickory nuts, some deer meat, some bear fat, and a little slippery elm ooze to make a concentrated energy food called pemmican. Elemental life at its best!

The slow-growing Persimmon tree, rarely a foot in diameter, belongs to the Ebony family. It is our northern representative of a mostly tropical family famed for its fruit and lumber. In the first wave of summer's hot weather, I become aware of the Persimmon by its thick sweet scent and the intense buzz of bees and other insects harvesting pollen from the male tree's waxy, bell-shaped white flowers. Persimmon can form dense patches, as it has done on my farm.

Beautiful in native settings and in plantings, the Persimmon has a striking trunk with black bark deeply checked into squares like plates. It has a noteworthy angular branch and twig formation. The leaves are glossy and the fruits are plum-like and turn a rich orange-red when fully ripe. If eaten early, before a frost, the fruit is so astringent it feels like your mouth has been turned inside out. Be patient. The ripened fruit becomes one of nature's sweetest, as sweet as dates, but with a custard-like texture. It is beloved by opossum, deer, raccoon, fox, many rodents, and birds.

The shiny flat oblong seeds make beautiful beads. Beer and brandy were made from its fruit, and the Persimmon's purple-black heartwood has Ebony's beauty and toughness. Like Dogwood, its heartwood was relied upon in the mills to take the strain and endless work of the loom shuttles. It was also the chosen wood at one time for the heads of golf clubs, as well as billiards cues. Its inner bark was used medicinally to treat intermittent fevers. I was once at a fall potluck, and one of my friends had made a Persimmon pie that was over-the-top good. I have never eaten one since.

Although primarily known for his bird paintings, one of my favorite of John Audubon's paintings is of a fruiting Persimmon tree with possum in it. Check it out.

Persimmon is content with the drier hillsides around here. Its beauty, strength, and giving nature should be appreciated by all, as it was by our First Nation people and early European explorers like Desoto and Captain John Smith, who recognized its vast food value. The Osage People of the Missouri River made bread called Staninca using the pulp of Persimmon pounded with corn into a flour. Sounds great!

Virginia Pine
Pinus virginiana
Pine Family
Scrub Pine

O f the few native pines in our area, Virginia Pine is an easy-going small, scrubby-looking pine. This species has given me wonderful results in my work reclaiming old strip mines. I have planted them and also witnessed first-hand, over time, their ability to move into these disturbed sights easily. I planted a five-acre area in an unreclaimed strip mine I bought for $350/acre twenty-eight years ago, and now have six hundred Virginia Pines that are doing just fine. On that site, Bigtooth Aspen *(Populus grandentata)* have now moved in to help the reclaiming process. I see that small Black Oaks are coming into the area now too. Just on the other side of the hill, I let the natural process continue, and I keep a trail open to observe the transition. Here, Virginia Pine is being helped by Black Locust, Blackberry, and Red Maple that are also moving in. It has been an incredible transformation from what I saw forty years ago, which was basically the moon with garbage. Another way I have been able to reclaim strip mine land is by turning them into beautiful hay fields, and I have been successful planting prairie grass into some of these sites. Why not plant strip mines back into prairie? Bird populations soar in prairie ecosystems, and the four-legged-ones love it.

Virginia Pines are short-lived and can break easily in storms. I have many standing in the old pastures and enjoy their rugged looks on the hillsides.

These pines pour forth sap where the branches break or have been pruned. The sap has antimicrobal and wound-healing properties, and can be incorporated into balms and salves, where it also lends its cleansing fragrance. I had a few storm-topped trees, almost 18 inches in diameter, and fairly straight—my neighbor, Paul Neidhart, milled them for me. The boards are an attractive light-orange color, knotty, and made a good-looking wall in the interior of a small barn. Virginia Pine can also be milled into quality two-by-fours for framing.

Like White Pine, deer browse saplings but happily, never seem to get them all. Chipmunk, squirrel, and birds feed on their seeds. Virginia Pine's bark has dark brown scaly plates bisected with red highlights. Its needles are two per bundle, 2-3 inches long, shiny, soft and flexible, and have a nice smell when crushed. Their seed cones are plentiful, 2-3 inches long, and broad near their base; they can hang on a tree for years. When you look at an older tree, many of the cones have the interesting feature of being bent backwards on their twigs.

Our Virginia Pine is an important pioneer species that paved the way for longer-lived forest species to continue the healing process of reforesting these strip-mined hills.

White Pine
Pinus strobus
Pine family

One of the most beautiful of all pines, the White Pine is widely distributed in the Northeastern United States and Canada, so the southeastern part of Ohio is in its range. Preferring well-drained soil and a humid climate, this is a tall, fast-growing, and long-lived tree. Twenty-two years ago I planted a White Pine seedling in my yard. A heavy winter storm with high winds, freezing rain and ice broke this beautiful tree in half. I was left with a 28 foot tall, 2 foot wide log with beautiful lumber to harvest. That's really fast growth for a tree of this young age.

White Pine have groups of five soft 2-4 inch long, soft slender needles that are blue-green with a white sheen. The whorl of branches ascending its trunk are most often in fives also. Each branch platform is a year in the tree's growth, so dating a White Pine is much easier than other trees, where you have to count core rings. Bark on young Whites is smooth and shiny, and becomes furrowed on older trunks. The tree is biennial-fruited, so it always carries two sizes of cones—older ripe cones are 5-8 inches long with thin broad scales, squaring at the tips, each scale containing two small seeds ¼-inch long. This food source is very important to wildlife. Many species of birds love it, while squirrels, chipmunks, and mice also eat these seeds. Beavers feed on the bark and twigs, and white-tailed deer browse its soft needles. Deer are the reason new plantings must be protected. Twenty-five years ago there were not as many deer and one didn't have to protect these young plantings as you must now.

Forming almost pure stands in our virgin forests, White Pine was the most abundant species throughout its northern range. Trees 150 feet tall, with 80 feet of straight, branchless trunk were common, and trees over 200 feet tall were not uncommon. A tree 240 feet in height was measured in Hanover, New Hampshire, at the site of Dartmouth College.

For hundreds of years, White Pine had no rival as a timber-producing tree. It was a keystone of our young country's development. White Pine was the earliest of our resources to be both used and abused. It was not just put to America's use; huge stands were also cut for export to England and also to Portugal, Spain, Africa, and the West Indies. It is the softest of the pines in eastern America, yet in proportion to its weight, it is extremely strong. Those old-growth trees were available in long lengths for ship's masts, becoming its main reason for export during this time. No other known part of the world had such a resource. Tropical timber is much too hard and heavy. The English had to piece together their masts with other woods, and, of course, were thrilled at this new resource when it was discovered. For them it was all about continuing their dominance of the seas. Besides selling mast wood to England, New England merchants figured out a "triangle trade." White Pine was exported to the Guinea coast of Africa, unloaded, and the boat was then loaded with African slaves sold into bondage in the West Indies. The boat was then loaded again in the Caribbean, this time with sugar and rum to sell in any Eastern seaport of the United States. From its earliest roots, America was invested in the horrific slave trade using White Pine as currency—blood money that helped build early New England fortunes.

The figureheads decorating the bows of New England sailing vessels were made with virgin White Pine, "so smooth and soft of grain that it could be cut with almost equal ease in any direction" (Donald Culross Peattie in *A Natural History of Trees of Eastern and Central North America*).

With good reason, the first flag of our revolutionary forces bore for its emblem a White Pine tree. One of England's first injustices against the American colonies was the English Crown's decree to reserve all the best specimens of White Pine for the Royal Navy. Choice standing trees were marked with a blaze known as the King's Broad Arrow, a symbol that infuriated the early pioneers.

After independence, the White Pine industry really took off. The vast stands of White Pine represented one of the greatest forest reserves on this planet, a rich natural resource for the Colonies. Powerful enough to affect the politics of the day, the logging lobby slowed the forces of conservation till most of the old growth was gone. "In 300 years of its exploitation, White Pine, more than any other tree in the country, built this nation literally and figuratively," writes Donald Paettie in *The Natural History of Trees*. White Pine was the most generally-used wood our nation has ever possessed.

For building purposes, White Pine was used in framing, flooring, shingles, window sashes, paneling, and furniture. From bobsleds to hobby horses, it proved itself effective for light, durable uses—and yet, matchsticks took a tremendous amount of White Pine's board feet every year. It was used in some parts of weaving loom production, and was also favored as a covered bridge material because of its durability and its lightness in proportion to its strength, the same characteristics that made it an ideal mast wood. Its wood built many of the bridges crossing the streams of Appalachia's original road systems.

Besides it sheer utility for humans and its food value for wildlife, it is also a wonderful medicinal plant. Today and as a young boy, I loved chewing White Pine needles. Turns out they are loaded with vitamin C and make a nice tea or tea ingredient. The inner bark of White Pine has long been used as a remedy for coughs and congestion, as a tea or as an ingredient in cough syrup. Its resinous sap can be used in salves and put into cold remedies and inhalants. Both the inner bark and the sap can be applied as a dressing for wounds.

White Pine is also used in the manufacture of turpentine, as a solvent, and in veterinary medicine also. Pine oil is manufactured for use in soaps and paints. As you can see, White Pine is a handy and beautiful tree to have nearby. In the autumn of the year, some of its needles turn brown and fall—I gather them as a wonderful smoker fuel for beekeeping and as mulch for acid-loving plants like blueberries.

Native American Plum
Prunus Americana
Rose Family

A small creek-way passes the walk up to the old farmhouse. Ever since I moved to the farm, this area has always been taken by our Native American Plum tree. It is a small, rapid-growing, but short-lived tree. It is common throughout Eastern and Midwestern America, growing along streams and the pastures and fence rows of abandoned farm land. Its bark is deep brown, exfoliating in little plate-like scales.

Every early spring, before its leaves are on, the plum patch becomes a mass of small, pure-white fragrant flowers for about a week. At this time, every bee and nectar-loving insect is upon it. When entering this halo of white on the walk coming up to the house you are greeted by a mass of energetic, loud buzzing. I always look forward to these days. The sweet welcoming aroma is one of nature's finest. A week later, the ground around the plums and the house garden is mulched white with plum petals. Spring is here! Time to get planting.

In late summer the American Plum carries a large crop of red-orange fruit. Besides people, the fruit is eaten by deer, fox, raccoon, squirrels, and many birds. In a good year, there are plenty to eat out of hand, and to make plum jam or plum butter. The fruit is about an inch long, its flesh is sweet and juicy, enclosing a flattened pit. The local Amish community appreciates this productive wild fruit and has taken the seed back to plant on their farms. Chipmunks especially love splitting open the plum pit and eating the kernel inside. I see them sitting on the old well cover beneath the Plum, cheeks bloated, shell casings all around them. Being a fruit tree, the Plum's wood is very hard and a pretty reddish-brown color, but much too small and curvy in shape to use for building. As it dies, I take the hot-burning firewood and think how lucky I am to live so close to such an enchanted entryway.

The Plum can be planted by seed. A mature one sends up sprouts that may be dug and re-planted. If you live on a farm, you will want to find a place to plant this giving tree. If it likes the chosen site, it will uncomplainingly provide beauty and food for all.

Eastern Redbud

Cercis canadensis
Fabaceae
Judas Tree

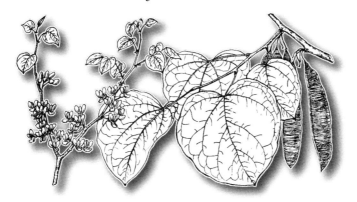

After forty-plus years of luscious springs on this farm, I carry deep in my heart the image of our beautiful Redbud in full rosy-purple flower riot in the richness of late April and early May. Redbud conveniently shares time and space with its mate, the Flowering Dogwood, and carpets of spring wildflowers. Both trees are signposts yelling, "Winter is done, spring is here now, rejoice!"

In Ohio, Redbud is generally a smaller understory tree that has also moved out into abandoned fields. The Redbud's trunk is gray-brown with scaly plates. Its wood is heavy and a deep red-brown. It is good firewood that can be taken when it dies or falls down.

Redbud flowers appear before the leaf and taste just wonderful alone and in salads. I encourage everyone to partake. Later, heart-shaped leaves cover the tree, concealing the Redbud's early seed pods. These pods then adorn the tree, rattling and rustling in the wind late into winter, giving this small tree another fine look and sound. The leaves are a lustrous deep green turning bright yellow in the fall.

Older Redbuds can be in a state of living and dying with both new growth and mature branches sharing the tree with older dead branches and trunks. Redbud trees are short lived, but can grow rapidly in favorable sites.

Redbud is easily transplanted and also flowers when very young, both wonderful qualities of this showy species. George Washington makes many notes in his diary of his Redbud plantings and their beauty at his Mount Vernon home.

Redbud is an insignificant food source for wildlife, and is insect-pollinated. Its red roots yield a dye. Redbud is also known as Judas Tree in the belief that Judas Iscariot hanged himself from the Eurasian species, *Cercis siliquastrum*.

April

At this very moment in April, on the acres around my house and cabin, the volume and diversity of life is so outstanding...a riot of flowering, mating, and nesting...shoots pushing their way to sunlight. It is the license of any normal April to run amuck. On the first of the month we get a snow and take a sweat with old friends. On the second it is 70 degrees, a good day to move manure. The Mourning Dove is on her eggs on the same beam in the tractor shed, and the yard is full of the Mockingbird's ever-changing song. Snakes awake, and much to my dismay it looks like a peak year for the tent caterpillar. First to be defoliated is the Wild American Cherry, my Apples are next. I help many Snapping Turtles and Box Turtles across the road. It has occurred to me often, that perhaps once, in every turtle's life, it must cross the road...a test of sorts in this speeding world. In other times, there were different tests.

By mid-April, all hell breaks loose and the flowering begins in earnest. Redbud, Dogwood, Spicebush, Pawpaw, Wild Ginger, Hepatica, Trillium, Violets, Geraniums, Dutchman's Britches, Peaches, and Cherries bloom. Black Cohosh, Goldenseal, Collinsonia, Ginseng, and Wild Yam break through the earth, and morels pop up. It is too dry to be a great morel year, but there are always some. The Sassafras is flowering as intensely as I have ever seen. Peas, lettuce, beets, carrots, spinach, kale, and taters are planted. Garlic is hoed. We watch a Scarlet Tanager bathe in Ramp Holler Creek in a pool of light.

Sassafras
Sasafrass albidum
Laurel Family

Before even Ginseng, Sassafras was the early American colonist's first herbal export and cash crop, our first international trade. Considered America's first "wonder drug," Sassafras filled the holds of large English sailing ships, becoming for a time England's favorite drink. In 1622, the Jamestown colony was committed by the Crown to produce 30 tons of Sassafras for export to England. The reverence for Sassafras is shown in the use of its wood for Bible boxes and cradles.

There are many striking features that will help you get to know this species. The taste and smell of Sassafras is totally unique, with no comparison amongst our American flora. The bark is noticeably reddish and gets blockier with age.

With the exception of Mulberry, there is no other tree here that has three distinctly-shaped leaves like Sassafras—that is, it bears three different leaf shapes. When leafing out in the late spring, Sassafras displays its flowering as a pale-gold candelabrum on naked branches. On a sky blue Indian summer day, in those weeks when there is no better weather and no better place to be than an eastern hardwood forest, Sassafras challenges even the Sugar Maple as autumn's biggest showoff. With brilliant reds, yellows, oranges, pinks, and purples all flaming on one tree for weeks at a time, Sassafras is truly amazing to behold. At leaf fall, you'll note its striking deep blue fruits on bright-red stems. The seeds are beloved by bluebirds, who deposit them on old fence rows, thereby increasing its range. Sassafras is a true pioneer species taking over and beautifying abandoned farmland.

In the past four years I have noticed more heart rot in our growing Sassafras population. Woodpeckers, especially the Pileated Woodpecker, glean the bugs (often carpenter ants) from its heartwood and create large nesting holes for themselves and other bird species. Another disease effecting Sassafras, also more prevalent in recent years, is the Nectria Canker. It is noticeable when branches fall and forms a concentric, or target-shaped (often diamond-shaped) wound that is rather attractive on the trunk. Decay rarely develops in wood underlying the canker. The disease spreads, so affected trees must be removed, as it may infect other hardwoods as well.

When doing trail work or hiking in hot weather, both Sassafras and Spicebush twigs moisten the mouth and help quench thirst. The leaves are a traditional herb in Creole cooking, its mucilaginous texture and spicy flavor being the key to a good gumbo filé.

Sassafras makes beautiful lumber. Though not strong, it is lightweight and durable. It has less shrinkage in the drying process than any other of our hardwoods. It is beautiful as siding and paneling and has been used for small boat building and fences. In the past, beds were made from Sassafras as were the roosts for chickens because of its ability to keep bed bugs and chicken lice at bay. The prevalent carpenter bees don't favor it, so it is great for facia, soffits, and siding. I love having access to so much Sassafras firewood. It splits easily and smells great, and burns super-hot. As a fire-starting kindling, or to get a fire cranking in the early morning, it is unsurpassed. Remember, it can pop and spark because of its high oil content.

Knowing of its reputation as a spring tonic, I associate my youth on this farm with the delight of digging and drinking Sassafras tea in March and April. When making Sassafras tea it is a common mistake to brew it too long; the longer it brews, the more bitter it becomes. A strong smell and a medium-amber color is enough. This is a good way to start to know this distinctive native tree.

The most active part of Sassafras is the root bark, which is a popular folk remedy for stomach aches, arthritis, rheumatism, kidney troubles, colds, fevers, skin eruptions, and gout. Sassafras may no longer be considered a "wonder drug" but surely is a wonder in all the valuable ways it gives. To anyone who has any amount of property, I suggest planting an abundance of this amazing tree. It does best on well-drained sites.

I am lucky to have such good soils, the real gold, on my farm. On a north-facing hillside with deep black loamy soil, above the Golden Healing Pond, Bill told me about three Sassafras trees, perfectly sound, six foot in diameter, that were cut out in the early 1950's. They were 80-100 feet tall with limbs starting 40 feet up the trunk. Trees like this do not exist here any longer.

While opening up a trail near this area, I found a dead-standing Sassafras three feet in diameter, 90 years old, the lumber still sound. With boards from this tree, I built the shelving for my tincture bottles in the Apothecary. That incredible smell was still in the wood. People from all over America come to this farm and are amazed by the amount and size of the Sassafras, but I know what it must have been like a hundred years ago, and I am sad that I missed it.

Sourwood
Oxydendrun arboretum
Ericaceae (Heath Family)
Sorrel Tree

Sourwood is the sole representative of its genus in the world, and we're lucky to have so many growing around us. It is a medium-sized tree that prefers well-drained, gravelly soils. Its beautiful, dark-colored bark is thick and deeply furrowed.

This species never seems to form pure stands. Though lovely in every season, the two most noticeable physical features of our Sourwood are its summer flowering and fall coloration. The small bell-shaped, upturned, creamy-white flowers look much like Lily of the Valley. They are mauled by honeybees and, when dry, remain on the tree through cold weather.

When the first hints of autumn come, Sourwood leaves turn a deep crimson, accenting our hills long before Oak, Sassafras, and Sugar Maple show their color. Sourwood honey is well known in Appalachia because of its tangy sweetness, and is considered one of the world's great honeys. This honey is normally found in areas where the trees grow naturally, where local demand buys up the entire crop at specialty prices.

In summer, Sourwood's beautiful shiny leaves are attractive and make a tasty thirst quenching nibble. This tree is a rare treat that goes unnoticed by most, except the deer that browse its leaves and twigs.

Sourwood is a hardwood that is rarely milled, but is great for tool handles. In pioneer days, its leaves were brewed as a tonic. If readily available, storm-damaged Sourwood makes good firewood. Because of its beauty, it is planted as a native ornamental and can adjust well to reclamation projects.

Spicebush
Lindera benzoin
The Laurel Family

Early spring and the leaves of our lovely multi-trunked Spicebush have not emerged, yet it is loaded with clusters of sweet, yellow, petal-less flowers. Spicebush is one of our earliest wild flowers and a dominant understory plant in our forests. Its beauty is clearly evident as it accents our hills and hollers in the new light streaming through a nearly leafless canopy. These flowers are an important source of energy for our emerging insect populations, and you can see why it is nicknamed the "Forsythia of the Forest."

During summer, Spicebush has dark green, waxy, un-toothed leaves that provide wonderful shade for woodland medicinals like Goldenseal, Ginseng, Cohoshes, and Trillium. It was used as an indicator of rich agricultural lands by early surveyors and farmers. By late summer into fall, shiny, scarlet barrel-shaped seeds cover Spicebush. Its leaves turning bright yellow is one of our last woodland color displays before cold weather sets in. Its berries can remain after leaf fall and are eaten by many birds, and is especially beloved by our sweet-singing Wood Thrush.

If you are lucky you can find the caterpillar of one of our biggest butterflies, the Spicebush Swallowtail, hidden amongst its leaves. It has a light-green to bright-orange body with four red eye-spots on its humped forepart.

Spicebush Swallowtail caterpillar

The Spicebush's aromatic twigs break easily. I use them to bring its spicy taste and moisture to my throat in hot weather. This taste is one of the identifying properties of the plant. The Cherokee Peoples used these twigs and leaves as a diphoretic and stimulating medicinal tea. The dried berries without seeds are powdered into a spice which tastes much like All Spice.

Our great local Snowville Creamery is planning to make a yogurt using these berries as a flavoring. The whole plant was used medicinally to bring on sweating, to break fevers, and to treat upper respiratory disease and colds. It can also help defend the body against colds. First Nation women used it to ease menstrual cramping. It can be taken as a tea for gas and colic, and in *Medicinal Plants and Herbs* by Steven Foster and James A. Duke, it is reported that the berries' oil can be applied to bruises, sore muscles, and joints. Duke also reports in his book *Herb-A-Day* that research is being conducted on using this plant to strongly inhibit yeast infections. I encourage you to try a light twig tea of this plentiful herb. Rebecca Wood's class came up with a great-tasting mix—50% Spicebush twigs and 50% White Pine needles, loaded with vitamin C.

Spicebush is related to Sassafras, and these are the only two members of the Laurel family represented on mesic sites in our eastern deciduous forest. Deer, rabbit, opossum, grouse, and many of our song birds eat the twigs and fruit.

It struck a resonant chord in me when reading Dr. Jody E. Noe's great article about Spicebush, "Tea That Makes Friends out of Enemies" in the United Plant Savers *Journal of Medicinal Plant Conservation*. I think about the culture I grew up in and ran from at an early age—an urban, white, sit-behind-a-desk world. Back then, I knew carrots were good for eyes, coffee was a stimulant, vegetables were good for me, and milk was good for strong bones…that's about it. That outlook is pretty narrow considering that without green plants this world would be nothing as we know it.

I quote Jody here in writing about Spicebush's medicinal benefits—regarding the sanity of a culture that not only uses raw plants as food and medicine, but as more:

"It is also used to make peace between two people, parties or clans, as well as a tea that is used to open up a conversation, a dialogue, or a gathering. The literal translation means, 'Tea That Makes Friends out of Enemies.' Once you have tasted the tea made from this plant, you will soon realize that it is a friendly tea."

Thank you for the reminder, Jody, that medicine can come in many forms. Kava has been used for thousands of years by native South Pacific people as a drink served before negotiations between disputing parties. There is so much our modern world needs to learn from its First Nation people. Congressman, Governors, Senators, Presidents everywhere—before leading this green world toward extinction and fiscal cliffs—should consider the common good for all, and not just humans. They should calm down and drink some Spicebush tea.

At morning feeding time on this January day it is 20°, clear, quiet with the welcoming, insulating silence of cold. Not even the birds are talking yet. The pleasant scent of wood smoke hangs in the still air with the dogs at my side… a moment of paradise. As a shield against the ever-quickening pace of time, I can finally recognize these rare and perfect moments in life… slow it all down, bathe myself in the present beauty, give thanks, and go back to task.

Entering the barn to get the sheep and donkeys their morning sweet-feed, I hear a steady crunching from a small hillside pasture I have just opened up for the animals to eat out the invasive Multiflora Rose and Autumn Olive. A week ago I watched the sheep just chewing down the thorny Multiflora, it doesn't have a chance, and anytime it sprouts they defoliate it. Same for the Autumn Olive. There is always a trade-off though, which I easily balance in this case because of the huge populations of Spicebush on the farm. As I round the corner, there is the entertaining sight of our two donkeys, Flora and Fauna, one on each side of a head-high Spicebush, eating three inch branch sections and just grinding them down—producing the only sound I was hearing that fine cold morning. And you know, I just have to hand it to those donkeys, knowing a good thing when they taste it. I suggest you also get to know this plant, it makes a great cover for our woodland medicinals.

Sycamore
Platanus occidentalis
Plantanaceae – Plane-Tree Family
Button Ball Tree

Our fast-growing American Sycamore is one of the more common trees in eastern North America. Though the Tulip Poplar is the tallest eastern forest hardwood, Sycamores have the most massive girth of any tree in our area. Hollow Sycamore trunks housed some early Appalachian families arriving new to these hills, sheltering them as they were building their farm houses.

The Sycamore is known for its splotched, peeling, and mottled bark. It grows an inner layer of bark each year and the outer bark, which does not grow, sheds off in large brown flakes toward the end of July. The inner bark—now the outer bark—becomes white as it is exposed to the sun.

The Sycamore's trunk is unique—multi-colored with brown, greenish-yellow, and white patches. Because Sycamores need water, they often grow along stream banks. By following their noticeable white upper branches, streams can be easily located. For the same reason, if you see a Sycamore high on a hill, you might have a spring nearby. You could use gravity to feed that water to an agricultural site below.

The one-inch fruit balls (button balls) dangle all winter long and, when spring arrives, they break apart into small brown parachute seeds. The Sycamore has little food value to wildlife; some rodents may feed on fallen seed.

Its leaf resembles a Sugar Maple's, being broad at its top with three main lobes. There is a hair or mold on the undersides of the Sycamore's new leaves that often sets me and others to sneezing. Interestingly, the hollow base of the leaf stem forms a protective cap over the developing winter bud. The wood's interlocking fibers make Sycamore ridiculously hard to split, which is the reason it was favored for butcher-blocks and ox yokes. Because its wood does not impart odor, taste, or stain to substances which it comes into contact with, it has also been used for small fruit and berry baskets. Quarter sawn, Sycamore wood makes beautifully-grained lumber that is used in furniture making by wood workers who know the beauty of "Lacewood."

Sycamore is a rapid grower and will sprout easily from its stump. Shoots can grow ten feet in the first season with leaves two times larger than normal. Sycamores are often planted in cities both for shade and its ability to withstand pollution. Because of its interesting look, it is an easy tree to recognize and appreciate.

Jim Sheets, a neighbor who grew up on Mud Fork Creek close to my farm in our Leading Creek Watershed, tells the story of a huge, hollow sycamore stump his father showed him many times saying, "One time, Jonah Coterill took his team of big draft horses inside the stump of this tree and could turn the horses around, and take them back out the way he took them in." I would have loved to have met that tree.

Tulip Poplar
Liriodendron tulipifera
Magnoliaceae - Magnolia Family
Yellow Poplar, Canoe Wood, Tulip Tree

Even though it is known as Tulip Poplar, this tree is really in the Magnolia family rather than the Poplar family. It stands alone in its genus in America.

There is no time of the year that the Tulip Poplar is not interesting and beautiful. It is one of the fastest growing of our hardwoods and attains the greatest height of any, with a trunk straight as a ship's mast. I have cut storm-damaged Tulip Poplars that are 2½ feet in diameter, but only 30 years old. It thrives in well-drained and rich soil and has been appreciated and planted in Europe since colonial times. Because of its height and symmetry, and because its branches begin so high up the trunk, the Tulip Poplar seems to soar from the earth right into the sky above. There are many groves of poplars in our forest, giving these areas a stately magnificence.

Young Tulip Poplar trees have a trim, smooth bark; older trees have a symmetrically grey, furrowed bark, with milky white in their valleys. Poplar leaves can never be mistaken for any of our other forest trees; they are distinctively square with two pointed lobes near the tip, and two to four lobes on the lower side. The leaves are five to six inches across. Long stemmed, they flutter in a breeze much like the ordinary poplar. The leaves turn a rich clear yellow in the fall.

162

Tulip Poplar leaf buds look like praying hands to me, and if you hold them up to the light, you can see as a shadow within its next curved leaf and petiole. The large showy tulip-shaped flowers appear after the leaves unfold; its petals are at first pale green, then yellowish with light-reddish inner markings. This 'bulls-eye' marking is a target for bees that dearly love the Tulip Poplar's thick nectar. In past years of heavy nectar flow, I have seen the blackening of Goldenseal leaves below, which is caused by the overflow of falling nectar. It took me a few days to figure out that the Goldenseal was not diseased but just being dowsed by the Tulip Poplar's sugary nectar. Cone-like clusters composed of closely-overlapping winged seeds develop and can remain on the tree through-out winter.

Being related to Magnolia, Tulip Poplar has a wonderful aromatic inner bark, which is one of my favorite forest scents, along with Sassafras of course. First Nation People used the bark tea to treat dysentery, fevers, digestive problems, and as a wash for wounds. At one time, the bark was used as a heart stimulant; a salve for burns was made from Tulip Poplar buds.

Tulip wood is soft, light, and easily worked, and was a favorite tree for native people to make canoes. Some of these canoes were large enough for a hundred people. Daniel Boone and his family, with all their sup-plies, paddled away from their old Kentucky home in a sixty-foot Tulip Poplar canoe.

Peeled Tulip Poplar bark makes utilitarian baskets. Early wells could be lined with its wood, as it imparts no taste to water. If growing in good soil, Tulip Poplar makes beautiful lumber. Log cabins were often built from its trunks. The siding on my 140-year-old house as well as my kitchen floor and Alana's solar cabin siding are all Tulip Poplar. This is a permaculture tree of many uses. It is a rapid grower and the stump sprouts when cut. Tulip Poplar is unique in that it is rarely browsed by deer. Cardinals, squirrels, rabbits and mice will feed on its seeds. It should be planted on every farm for its beauty and for future use.

Tulip Poplar can be used in place of old growth lumber coming from Canada and the west coast. For much of my lumber needs, I am able to thin some of the thick stands that have taken over 60-year-old pastures on my farm.

In this herbal forest I live in, it is obvious that if you have lots of Tulip Poplar you have a whole lot of medicinal herbs. Many of the Tulip Poplars planted at George Washington's home in Mount Vernon, Virginia are still standing today. These were planted for shade and beauty for the many large gatherings the Washingtons would have during the heat of the summer, when their home was much too hot to be indoors. In Europe, the Tulip Poplar tree is one of the most popular of all American species and has been planted there since the mid 1600's.

Isn't life interesting? In the summer of 2012's high heat, all of the Tulip Poplar in our area were devastated by Poplar Scale. This organism sucks the tree's juices and excretes a super-sweet liquid that blackens all below as it dries. Maybe what I saw years ago was a small, localized Poplar Scale outbreak, and not the sloshing of overfilled flowers swaying in the breeze. It is obvious we could use some really cold winter weather this year. I have noticed many sapling Tulip Poplars die this year, smothered by their mother's insect-secreted juices.

"The tulip-tree, high up,
Opened, in airs of June, her multitude
Of golden chalices to humming-birds
And silken-winged insects of the sky."
—William Cullen Bryant, *The Fountain,* St. 3

Tupelo
Nyssa sylvatica
Tupelo Tree Family
Black Gum

A wide-ranging deciduous species found from eastern Texas north to Maine and south to northern Florida, Tupelo or "Black Gum" is abundant in the Ohio River Valley. Yet in our forests it is never as populous as our Oaks, Ash, Hickory, Beech, Maples or Tulip Poplars.

Like Tulip Poplar, Tupelo's trunk can run mast-straight. Its short branches are noticeably horizontal to the trunk, eventually drooping as they grow. Its popular name, Black Gum, refers to its dark bark, which is broken into many-sided small plates. It's straight stature, horizontal branching and unique bark patterns make this tree easy to identify, and a pleasure to look at. I have yet to find the reason for "Gum" in its common name, except in the term Bee Gum.

Tupelo's flowers are small and greenish, and appear in the spring when the leaves are partially grown. The ovate, alternate, and lustrous dark green leaves are leathery to the touch. They are two to four inches long. In spring the leaf buds have a similar scarlet color to the leaves in their early fall magnificence. And in fall, much of the forest still has green leaves when

Tupelo's leaves turn to that brilliant scarlet splendor. A feast for the eyes, it marks the early fall season.

Tupelo's autumn fruit hangs from long drooping stalks. It is fleshy, about 1 ½ inches long, dark blue almost black, and bitter-tasting. Its egg shaped seed has a prominent ribbed surface. This fruit is much too bitter to be eaten by humans out of hand, but is a food source for turkeys, wood ducks, opossums, woodpeckers, and for many of our song birds. I watched a flock of robins glean its fruit on a cold, late October morning. Deer browse the twigs and foliage.

Tupelo is not a long-lived tree like our Oaks. Decay sets in early, usually beginning at the top. The rot usually affects the heartwood, so hollow trees are common. The wood decays quickly when in contact with the soil. Before the tree gets hollow, its wood is extremely tough and almost impossible to split because of its twisted grain. For these attributes, it was made into tool handles and wooden parts for farm machinery.

Before our modern beehives and removable frame systems, hollow sections of Black Gum would be cut into short sections for beehives. This is why the old name "Bee Gums" is used for hives. Back then, longer hollow sections were also fashioned into rabbit traps.

I recently saw Civil War-era Bee Gums at a roadside museum and store in Pocahontas County, West Virginia. The Bee Gums were good-sized, about three feet high and two feet in diameter, the hollow bee space about one and a half feet wide. Sticks were placed on the inside for bees to build their comb. A board was used for the hive bottom, with a cutout for the entrance put in the bottom of the Bee Gum. And then a board was simply used for its top. I imagine they would last a long time if placed under the roof of a southeast-facing barn shed. When full, the hive was smoked and combs of honey were pulled out and sliced in a colander and placed over a pot on a warm day to drip out. This was simple honey extraction before the advent of modern centrifugal extractors and uncapping knives. The wax, drained of honey, could then be made into candles.

A southern variety of Black Gum known as Water Tupelo *(Nyssa aquatica)* makes one of America's most famous honeys. The bee yards are put on platforms above the swamps where the bees gather prodigious amounts of honey. Remember Van Morrison's great song "Tupelo Honey"? This specialty honey has a different makeup of sugars, with a much higher percent of levulose to dextrose, so it rarely becomes solidified. It is said that it is more easily tolerated by folks with blood sugar disorders than any other honey, but I cannot verify that.

Bees

Beekeeping as a winter job near New Smyrna Beach, Florida in 1975, I helped unload and extract a semi-truck load of Southern Tupelo honey. This warehouse alone held a million pounds of honey. In this kind of large-scale commercial beekeeping, with its high-volume automation of uncapping and extraction, the honey is heated so much that it kills many of its healthful properties. While heated, it is forced through banks of filters on its way to the bottling conveyor belts. Quality is sacrificed for speed. Small producers do not need to do this kind of heating, and physical filtration is minimal. This is the honey you want. On that job, I did save five pounds for myself before it got heated. It had an interesting color, being golden with a greenish cast. I also saved a frame to keep for its comb honey. It was very beautiful because of the pure white comb. The driver of the semi told me that the flow was so heavy, some of the hives were putting out a hundred pounds of sealed honey a month.

In the large orange groves where I worked bees that winter, it was possible to get thirty pounds of sealed Orange Blossom honey a week! Bees work our forest's Black Gums, but around here, in Ohio, the trees are not plentiful enough for us to extract pure Tupelo Honey.

Black Walnut
Juglans nigra
Walnut Family

Along with Basswood, Black Walnut was originally one of the most common trees in the Ohio Valley. A majestic tree, Black Walnut grows best in rich, moist, well-drained soil. Trees 150 feet tall, with branches starting at fifty feet, were not uncommon in our old growth forests. But it is shade intolerant and needs many feet of top soil to grow successfully.

Black Walnut is one of our most amazing plants and provides food, medicine, and building materials. Because Walnut is one of the finest lumber trees in North America, it has always been in high demand. Black Walnut has been over-cut in most of its native habitat, and needs protection to ensure the future of this giving tree. So much has been lost!

Walnut is late to leaf out in the spring and loses its leaves before most other trees in the fall. Its stately, almost black, deeply furrowed trunk make it easy to identify, even without leaves. In the summer months, its alternate compound leaves, 1-2 foot long with 15-23 leaflets, are a lustrous green yellow and gracefully dance even in the slightest breeze. Another key to its identification are the crushed leaves that give a spicy, acrid smell unique only to Walnut. After the leaves fall, its round nuts remain hanging. Squirrels are the main distributors of its nuts. Being a delicious and nourishing food source, there is a large market for these nuts. To help support myself in the early years on this farm, I would gather walnuts to sell to bulk buyers in Pomeroy every fall. At the time, most of these nuts went to flavor Black Walnut ice cream.

Walnut hulls leave a deep brown stain on the hands that even soap won't clean off. Once taken off the nuts, the hulls make a superior alkaline compost. Containing the chemical juglone, Black Walnut is allelopathic (inhibiting the growth of other plants). Black Raspberry does not seem to mind it, but Blackberry does. I have found Goldenseal under its spreading limbs, and grasses don't seem to be intimidated either. Obviously, juglone is plant-specific and as many plants seem to thrive in walnut shade as avoid it. That said, I know you do not want it near your gardens. Interestingly, the allelopathic effect of Walnut seems to inhibit other Walnut trees—they seem to enjoy their own company and stand alone without their own as close neighbors.

Black Walnut is a major medicinal herb and can be used in many ways. In our hot humid summer months I successfully use a green walnut hull tincture for athletes' foot. It destroys most funguses and has been used successfully for Candida. Containing iodine, the leaf makes a good wound wash. It has also been used to balance hypothyroidism. Along with blood root, it is successful against ring worm. Black Walnut makes a good gargle for hoarseness and sore throat, and is also used for dandruff, eczema, internal ulceration, worms, and hemorrhoids. In addition, it is a wonderful dye plant that doesn't require a mordant; it gives different shades of rich browns. It is a great food source and the nuts can be pressed into high-quality oil.

Walnut has always been used in more expensive grades of cabinets, furniture, paneling, and veneer. Its wood is strong but not heavy, a deep brown with purple highlights that has a beautiful luster and grain when polished.

When researching Black Walnut I found that large amounts of the trees were felled during WWII for use as gunstocks under the government's "make your trees fight" campaign. It seems that Walnut is light and smooth to the touch, yet tough, helping to cushion recoil. Most importantly, it doesn't splinter when hit by gunshot. When in contact with the soil, the heartwood of Walnut is very durable and was valued for fence posts and door sills, shingles and log cabins.

This is a tree of so much beauty and usefulness that it has been over-harvested far too long. Having so many attributes and being of high monetary value, anybody on a large farm or small homestead should consider planting Black Walnut for the future.

In 1978, when clearing a north-facing hillside for pasture, I left all of the Redbuds, Dogwoods, and Black Walnut in place. These Walnuts are doing okay. They have never been bothered by any of my livestock, including sheep, horses, donkey, cattle, mules, and goats for the past 35 years. My thought then, which I have since put into my will, was that any member of my family running this farm could harvest 50% of these trees if a financial emergency arose.

Plant this tree in a sandbox with wire mesh on top and bottom to protect against rodent and squirrel thievery. In the sandbox, place the nuts to stratify throughout the winter. In late spring, the sprouts can be transplanted to large tree pots or tree tubes to be planted the following year.

Willow Family
Black Willow *Salix nigra*
Weeping Willow *Salix babylonica*
Coyote or Basket Willow *Salix exigua*
Sandbar Willow *Salix interior*
Missouri Willow *Salix eriocephala*

There are many varieties of Willows in our area. Some seventy species are native to North America, but only twenty-four become tree-sized, the others being shrubs. Willows are short-lived sun lovers and they hybridize easily. They are fast-growing and live near water courses. Their lance-shaped leaves come on late in spring, and yellow leaves can hang on into late fall.

Willows have a light and flexible wood that is used for baskets and furniture and, in Holland, for wooden shoes. You can take a Willow branch and place it in wet dirt and it will root. I make a rooting water for plant propagation by placing many stems of Willow in warm water in the sun for a few days. I use this "willow water" to soak any plant that I am rooting. Sometimes I find willows in field sites and of course this would be a good spot for a water hole or small pond.

Easy-bending Willows make great sweat lodges and wikiups. They are a wonderful shade tree in the proper locations and are an important source of browsing food for wildlife. Salicin, found in Willow bark, is nature's aspirin; it can be used for pain reduction, inflammation, headaches, arthritis, fevers, and toothaches. The leaves can be used as a poultice for sores and sprains, and can be combined with Witch Hazel for this purpose.

On some of our willows you can see "Willow Roses." These are not fruits, but the result of a sting from an egg-laying insect on the terminal Willow buds. In Main Holler Creek, just below the big barn at the United Plant Savers Botanical Sanctuary, you can see are many of these Willow Roses. They make wonderful dried arrangements.

Weeping Willow is one of the first trees I knew as a child. I think this is true for many youngsters, which makes this species a great entry point into appreciating and knowing the "big herbs." Sit down in its shade and watch the waters go by, listen to nature's sound moving all around you. As William Blake noted, "Life delights in life."

Willows are a good species for erosion control, and are commonly used for stabilizing stream banks. They must be managed in small farm pond situations because they can reproduce so fast in a good habitat that they will quickly dominate, making the pond smaller and dirtier, and also eliminating other species you may want. I use my ponds for gravity irrigation, fish and amphibian habitat, stock watering, and recreation. If needed in a drought, pond water can be filtered and used in the farm house. I have no use for city water, and gravity never fails, never costs, can make electricity, and feels good.

As part of my farm management in the fall of the year, I pull out all of the Willow sprouts I find. Even a small Willow sprout can have a surprisingly large root system. They are much easier to pull earlier than later.

Simplicity is one of the keys of life, especially in a world going mad at an ever-faster pace. What is all the rush about?

Witch Hazel
Hamamelis virginiana
Snapping Alder
Witch Hazel Family

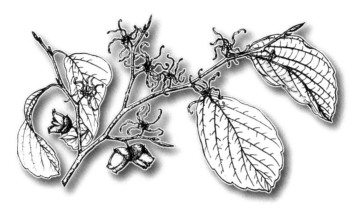

Witch Hazel is a many-stemmed understory shrub, though it can also be brought out into light. It grows in mesic to dry woodlands or along their edges. It has rough unsymmetrical alternate leaves, 3-6 inches long, with an uneven round to wedged-shaped base. The leaves turn a beautiful yellow in autumn and often persist until spring.

Uniquely, around here this plant will only start flowering after frosts from September to December. Tiny buds the size of a pinhead open into starry blossoms with thin, twisted, ribbon-like yellow gold petals; the scent of these flowers can be mesmerizing. At the same time Witch Hazel is flowering, its previous year's seed pods are opening up and ejecting their seeds up to twenty feet with an audible snapping, hence the nickname "Snapping Alder." You can see how this can be a beautiful and exciting landscaping plant. Squirrels and some birds feed on Witch Hazel seed and deer browse its young branches and leaves.

First Nation people used its leaves, twigs, and bark as an astringent for treating inflammations. An extract of the plant is used as a wash or aftershave, and is sold in most pharmacies. It can also be used for bruises and sprains. Witch Hazel branches are one of the preferred species used as a divining rod to find water, also known as "witching for water."

Over the years I have planted many different varieties of Witch Hazel in both open and semi-shaded sites. They are all doing well and all of them are a joy to live with. All mature Witch Hazels have young trees that sprout from their seed near its base. These can be dug up with an intact earth ball and easily transplanted, or given away to others who will also fall for the charms of this small tree.

This is a wonderful landscaping tree for those who don't have much light in their yard. Try planting a little Goldenseal and Trillium underneath it.

Part III
—*Maintaining Sanctuary*—

Illustration by Wendy Minor Viny

8

Death Comes Knocking

Strange weather can have alarming consequences for an ecosystem. The fall of 2002 was unusually hot and dry. It is a rare occurrence to have such dry streambeds at this time of year, but that is what was needed to hatch out a tiny gnat whose bite infected our sizable deer herd with the disease E.H.D. (Episodic Hemorrhagic Disorder). Within a two-month period I find twenty-seven dead deer on the farm and Sanctuary alone. I watch three young deer wobble and drop dead right in front of me. Many of the carcasses I find next to fence lines; they didn't have the energy to jump over. Their inner organs hemorrhage and they bleed to death. Thin bodies blow open in two days and even the dogs, who dearly love deer meat at almost any phase of decomposition, will not touch it. Old and young alike are affected. I find the rack and skull of a stately 10-point buck just below the Cave of the Fallen Cow. I know this natural, yet rare, occurrence has likely had some benefits to the area—a thinning out of the old and weak. Low populations allow new deer to move into the recently-vacated area, giving more genetic variations. I am sure that there are many positive effects that I am not aware of.

What will remain with me so strongly from this event was the cloying smell of death that hung around for a month. A smell that colored everything, ever present and overpowering, no place to run and hide, death walks the hills and is contained in all.

I can now relate to those who speak of the horror of battlefields littered with dead. Smell is so very powerful, able to dredge up otherwise held-back thoughts and memories—of forgotten times. For me, these are most often wonderful because of the rich, sweet, plant smells all around. Pay attention, smell can be an invisible key to unlocking our past.

It's deer season, and a little more than a year removed from the die-off. What I have noticed, but more importantly, what Little Lee and the other hunters who have hunted here since their youth have noticed, is that populations have recovered some—most of this a result of transient or button bucks filling in. They have also noticed that there is an unusually low population of fawns this year. It is suspected that many does that made it through the die-off may have aborted.

I still see plenty of deer, but lower populations might lead to higher Ginseng numbers. Not a bad trade.

Ramp Holler in late March—the ground covered with ramps

—9—
"What Doesn't Kill You Makes You Stronger"
The 2003 President's Day Ice Storm

The notes in my calendar call it a day of beautiful devastation—a natural occurrence for sure, a pruning of weak trees, the making of future forest soil. But if you love trees, and already had more than enough work, it was devastating! Yet another hundred-year set of weather circumstances I get to see, feel, clean up, and remember.

A cold snowy February day warms up. The snow turns to sleet, and then rain, and then it turns real cold again. Every living and non-living thing is totally coated with inches of glimmering ice—a mythological valley of glass and intense refractive light. The fields, already covered with five inches of snow, get another three inches of ice. Walking becomes laborious crunching and for twelve hours, the sound of creaking, cracking, crashing, and popping takes over the world. Trees and tree tops fall everywhere. Ice war has come to the forest and farm.

Gutters twisted, slate roofs partially destroyed, electric lines down. Electric service being out for twelve days is the least of my worries. To clean up just the area around my cabin and camp kitchen, to get it ready for spring classes, takes twelve guys, four chainsaws, and ten hours of work.

Days of chain sawing has so warped my brain that I had an early morning dream in which my arms turned into chainsaws, my mouth a chipper, chips shooting out of my ass as I scream madly. But I am an herbalist, after all. And the endless cleaning up of three miles of forest trails and a half-acre of medicinal herb beds begins. The work takes months and then it's time for a summer of salvage logging. Plans change.

All of you who may idealize, or want the life of a farmer or herbalist, responsible for large tracks of land, please know that it comes with a dangerous reality most people would never want to deal with. Work, joy, madness, and sadness can make a confusing mix; in the end everything is out of your control. You learn the limits of your land and yourself. In the end, I am no more than this land's groundskeeper, a temporary cog in this Earth's wheel, perfect yet dirty, as soil is slowly and silently built for the forest's future.

As time passes, the memory of the work and devastation will dim. What I will carry to my death is the ungodly sounds of a forest giving part of itself up, in the end, to enrich the whole. All is change. What doesn't kill you, makes you stronger.

Post-icestorm spectacle at Golden Healing Pond

Heart Pond
United Plant Savers Botanical Sanctuary

Named Heart Pond for its distinct heart shape when viewed from the opposite west-facing hill, this was the last of eight ponds I built between 1979-1993. I specifically designed Heart Pond to supply water by gravity to the fields, green house, gardens and yurt below it, even during drought years, using no pumps or electricity.

Heart Pond creates a wonderful swimming hole in our hot summers and a fun fishing pond that Little Lee keeps stocked. There are two separate yet interconnecting water filters in the pond; one of them is the visible floating grey dome. The other is a barrel filter placed at the bottom. All water lines are two inches for maximum volume. I also made a channel at the bottom with hollow tiles to encourage fish breeding.

When we dug 25 feet down, we found a rich vein of limestone below the pond, indicative of the ancient ocean that once covered this land. These are now the giant limestone blocks that make up the pond's table and chairs. Some are placed on the beach area and one is used as the outdoor table at the yurt. If you look at the tabletop, you can see shell fossils—evidence of millions of years of compressed life.

Ponds support and magnify life: wood ducks live here, Canadian geese and mallards nest here, deer drink here, a raccoon washes its food here. The lovely water plant *Ludwigea* (Seed box) floats its young on these waters. The great blue heron fishes these waters as dragonflies lay their eggs in calm corners. Our native hibiscus, Swamp Rose Mallow, blooms beside the beach.

With the help of Hank H. and Paul N., we seeded a prairie on the hillside opposite the beach as well as the field below. These native prairies support a large variety of insects and bird species. It's all a circle, all connected, but the start and end is always water.

Flow well friends.

Heart Pond is dedicated to my loving friend Little Lee's dad, Lee Oaky Wood, whose good works and open mindedness to the wild ideas of a young man made Heart Pond possible.

Illustration by Wendy Minor Viny

Creating Botanical Sanctuaries
by Christopher Hobbs L.Ac., RH (AHG) and Rosemary Gladstar

Y*ou can create a botanical sanctuary on any amount of land… a city lot, a backyard, or—on the other extreme—with 700 acres of forests and fields. Which is exactly what Paul Strauss, herbalist-farmer, did. Three decades of keen observations and commitment to the land has instilled in him a knowledge deeper than any amount of book learning. In the early 1970s, Paul settled on a small farm in Southeastern Ohio. Land purchase and stewardship became an overriding passion as his relationship with the land developed. Unable to sit back and watch as the surrounding forests were clear cut, displacing the plants and animals that live there, Paul mobilized friends, family and community members to purchase land. Over 700 acres of farmland and forest were preserved in the ensuing years. Strip mines that had devastated the land were reclaimed, the land re-planted, and ponds put in. The sanctuary evolved naturally as Paul replanted, restored, and reclaimed the land.*

In 1998, Paul donated seventy acres of his land to United Plant Savers to help form the first UpS Botanical Sanctuary. Shortly thereafter, Michael and Judy Funk of Mountain People, a natural products distributor, made a considerable donation that enabled UpS to buy three-hundred adjoining acres, completing the first United Plant Savers Botanical Sanctuary. This 370-acres farm has many of the elements of a plant sanctuary already in place. The land is 50% mature diverse native hardwood forest and 50% fields. Extensive botanical assays have been performed to determine the resources present on the land. To date, over five-hundred species of plants, over one-hundred-twenty species of trees and over two hundred species of fungi have been identified. Half of the "UpS At Risk" native medicinal plants are thriving in abundance on this land. Large communities of Goldenseal, American Ginseng, Black and Blue Cohosh, and grand old medicinal trees species such as White Oak and Slippery Elm flourish on this reclaimed land. The UpS Sanctuary is a living model for protecting diversity and ensuring that the rich traditions of North American and Euro-American folk medicine continue to thrive.

But one doesn't need a large parcel to steward land to create a Sanctuary. UpS Advisory Council member Katherine Yvinskas has created a different and equally-valuable model of a Botanical Sanctuary in her backyard in Morris County, New Jersey. In this small plot, Katherine has created an enchanted sanctuary for plants and people. Her garden landscape is planted in natives, and in a wooded corner of her lot she has planted several at-risk herbs. Goldenseal, American Ginseng, Blue and Black Cohosh, Mayapple, and Bloodroot are thriving where the former owners grew only grass. Amidst her community, Katherine's botanical sanctuary offers a quiet respite for the weary, a reflective place to ponder, a joyous gathering spot to share with friends, and an educational center where others come to learn about the medicinal uses of native plants. Even on this small plot, Katherine is able to offer workshops and herb walks to raise her community's awareness of native plant conservation.

She's planning her sanctuary to be a welcoming spot for others besides the two-legged. By simply installing a birdbath and a small pond, an increase in birds, butterflies, and bees was noted in the first season. Reflecting on her Sanctuary, Katherine explains, "The sanctuary reflects my love affair with the Dao, the complementary forces of nature. There is an ebb and flow to the garden. To me, it's living sculpture, always changing, beautiful to watch as it unfolds season by season. I feel blessed. The garden sanctuary is truly paradise… am I in heaven?"

Rosemary Gladstar, president and founder of United Plants Savers, created yet another model of sanctuary. Living in the midst of thousands of acres of wilderness in the Green Mountains of Vermont, Rosemary became acutely aware of the necessity of maintaining the integrity of the wilderness and the importance of protecting large 'green belts' for wild life and plant preservation. When a 100-acre parcel of old growth forest abutting Sage Mountain, Rosemary's 500-acre Retreat Center and Botanical Sanctuary, was slated for clear cutting, Rosemary appealed to friends and family for help. Through a lengthy and complex transaction, the land was purchased by the Friends of Hannah Hill and placed in a UpS land trust with strict conservation easements ensuring it will remain 'forever wilderness.' The old growth forest, home to black bear, moose, white tailed deer, and beaver as well as a rich variety of native plants, remains in its pristine state.

But the story doesn't end there. In talking with surrounding landowners, Rosemary found a great deal of interest in land preservation. Several other landowners in the area are considering placing large tracts of land in 'forever wilderness' conservation easements. A small community-supported nature center is being built, and a mile-long, self-guided Medicine Trail has been established. It has become a popular place for community members to hike, to learn about the native plants and wildlife, and to become more aware of habitat preservation and plant conservation.

The possibilities are infinite. All it takes is people willing to make a difference. Whether you have a small backyard like Katherine, a working farm like Paul, or a tract of wilderness, imagine it as a sanctuary, a haven for plants, wildlife, and people. The concept of ownership of land was unheard of by native people. How could one own land, own the heart of the mother earth? We are stewards of the land, caretakers in the deepest sense of the word. By creating sanctuary, we begin to restore the idea that land belongs to all life, that it is life, and that our job is to restore it to its richest diversity.

Growing Awareness
The Practical Side of A Botanical Sanctuary
Once you decide to establish your own botanical sanctuary, what practical steps can you take to help it grow and flourish, and be of service? Focus on these four areas: Identification, Restoration, Preservation, and Education.

⋆ Learn to identify plants
Before this century, herbalists were also botanists. Begin by identifying as many plant species on the land as possible. Invite a friend over that knows some of the plants, and buy several identification guides. When we moved onto our forty-acre piece in the Soquel hills near Santa Cruz, California, I roamed the land observing every plant and tree. As I recognized the plants, one by one, I began a list which eventually grew to over two-hundred species. For the eastern United States, I recommend the Peterson Field Guide to Medicinal Plants of the Eastern U.S. by Steven Foster and James Duke. Terry Willard wrote an identification guide to Rocky Mountain medicinal plants, and Michael Moore's excellent books cover the western U.S. Many flower identification books offer full color photos specific to your area and are available at your local

bookstore or local wildflower society. For the more technically-minded, order a flora, or technical identification manual, for your bioregion or state.

★ Learn where plants come from and where they are going

Pay special attention to whether a plant is native to your area, an ornamental from some exotic place, or a weedy species. Many weedy plants, though valuable and often lovely to look at, tend to take resources like water and light that native plants require to live. In establishing a botanical sanctuary, you will want to limit the number of weedy species that thrive on your land, especially if they are obviously widespread. Herbalists love dandelion and milk thistle, which are valuable medicinal plants, but try to limit their growth to specific areas. One of the first things I did on our land in the Santa Cruz Mountains was to establish a good weed patch. I collected weedy seeds and plants from all over the county and actually brought them to the land; first, because I love their tenacity and survivability, and second, so I could observe them more closely and begin to understand how they fit into the whole botanical tangle. I removed many other weedy plants around the land, especially in those areas/habitats that were most conducive to the native wild species. Don't forget about the UpS consultant service. We can put you in touch with a consultant who can help you learn more about your ecosystem and how to go about establishing and managing a sanctuary.

★ Plant Natives

Identify as many plants and trees that originally came from your ecosystem as possible. The more you learn about the ecosystem where you live, the better able you will be to help the land regenerate. In the processes, you will be renewed and regenerated. Get to know your land intimately. Wander all over it and, with permission, the surrounding areas. Get your neighbors involved! Locate a local native plant nursery or wildflower society. Whenever possible use local sources. This preserves the purity, precedents, and intelligence of the original ecosystem where you live. You can order the same species from a supplier or nursery, but these may be genetic hybrids or carry the genes of some other species. We do a lot of seed collecting and propagation through cutting of local plants. I carry those little brown coin envelopes with me all the time to store, identify, and organize weedy and native seeds. These are available from a craft store or stationary store.

185

⋆ Preserve and protect the land

Join the UpS Sanctuary network, and be your own sanctuary manager. In today's world, the land needs a champion, a steward, and a manager to reduce interference, to bring natives back to the land, and allow the intelligence of nature to work her magic. Signs are available through UpS that can be hung around the perimeter of your land to help people honor and preserve the sanctuary.

⋆ Allow your Sanctuary to become the educational center it naturally is

Teaching and learning about the land is a lifetime study. Within every community you'll find knowledgeable people who are often willing to share. Invite them to your land. And always be willing to share with others what you have learned about land management, wild plants, and the importance of biodiversity.

⋆ Create a medicine trail

on your land as part of your educational effect. It can be a path through your front yard, or as on Rosemary's land, a self guided mile long trail. Make signs or have them made that provide the Latin binomial, common name, origin, and uses of the plants on the trail.

⋆ Lead herb walks

or encourage others to give classes on the land. You'll often find knowledgeable and willing people through the local forestry service, wildflower societies, herb clubs, and sometimes senior citizen clubs.

⋆ Create a nature center on your land

Teach others how to grow wild plants, ethical wildcrafting techniques, preservation, medicine-making, and herbal therapeutics.

⋆ Help create and preserve serene places among the plants and trees for communion with the green spirits and divas.

With my first two Ohio University botany boys, Andy and Dave, and a May morning harvest headed to the Athens Farmers Market.

Bibliography

The Book of Forest and Thicket by John Eastman, Stackpole Books, 1992

The Complete Trees of North America by Thomas S. Elias, Random House Value Publishing, 1987

Some American Trees by William B. Werthner, Macmillan, (out of print), 1935

The Go-to Book and Perfect Bathroom Reader for Tree Lovers by Donald Culross Peattie, Houghton Mifflin, 1991

American Canopy by Eric Rutkow, Scribner, 2012

Manual of the Trees of North America (Two Volumes) by Charles Sprague Sargent, Dover, 1961

Much of the information in this book I have accumulated by working with or talking to folks whose lives revolve around farm and forest.

Contacts

For products from Equinox Botanicals—www.equinoxbotanicals.com

For the film, *The Sanctity of Sanctuary: Paul Strauss and the Equinox Farm,* a film by Blis Hanousek DeVault—www.sanctityofsanctuary.com

For United Plant Savers—www.unitedplantsavers.org

For U.p.S. internships—call 740-742-3455

For more of Wendy Minor Viny's artwork—Ohio Arts Council AIE artist, at http://www.oac.state.ohio.us/search/aie/ArtistsDirectory/ http://www.instagram.com/wendyviny# and instacanv.as/wendyviny http://www.theydrawandtravel.com/maps/the-green-corridor-rutland-ohio-wendy-minor-viny

Index

191

192

197

198

199

200

201

BYRON BAY
INTERNATIONAL
FILM FESTIVAL
AUSTRALIA
BEST
ENVIRONMENTAL
FILM

ENVIRONMENT,
HEALTH & CULTURE
INTERNATIONAL
FILM FESTIVAL
INDONESIA
HONORABLE
MENTION

CINCINNATI
FILM FESTIVAL
BEST
REGIONAL
FILM

ATHENS
FILM FESTIVAL
OFFICIAL
SELECTION

MAUI
INTERNATIONAL
FILM FESTIVAL
OFFICIAL
SELECTION

BAHAMAS
INTERNATIONAL
FILM FESTIVAL
OFFICIAL
SELECTION

PAUL STRAUSS & THE EQUINOX FARM

To order your copy, log or
www.sanctityofsanctuary.

An Appalachian love affair
between a man, his farm
and his desire to
make the world a
better place

The Sanctity of
Sanctuary

A film by Blis Hanousek DeVault | www.sanctityofsanctuary.com